THE PROVINCIAL ASYLUM IN TORONTO

REFLECTIONS ON SOCIAL

AND

ARCHITECTURAL HISTORY

Editor: Edna Hudson

TORONTO REGION ARCHITECTURAL

CONSERVANCY

TORONTO

Canadian Cataloguing in Publication Data

The Provincial Asylum in Toronto
Reflections on social and architectural history

1. Architecture, Modern – 19th century Canada. 2. Architects – Canada – Biography.
3. History – mental health, Ontario. 4. History – Ontario

ISBN 0-9699054-3-2

The cover is a composite featuring, centre front, watercolour and ink drawing,
attributed to W. J. Thomson 1890, see p. 166. Background and detail on back cover is
from oil on canvas painting by E.T. Dartnell 1851, Panoramic View of the City of
Toronto. ROM

Printed in Canada.

IN MEMORY OF

B. NAPIER SIMPSON, Jr.,

23 May 1925 - 23 June 1978

. CONTENTS .

ACKNOWLEDGEMENTS

IT IS WITH PLEASURE we acknowledge a grant from the Jackman foundation, to help with the costs of illustrations, and a generous donation from the McLean Foundation. This support set the project on a serious footing, and was most useful and timely.

Cyril Greenland has been advisor and friend to the project from the beginning. It could not have continued through its long incubation stage without his steadfast interest. He has also been a reader of most of the papers.

Many archivists, librarians and historians have been instrumental in the completion of this work. Particularly important have been the contributions of staff at: the Archives of Ontario (Christine Bourolias); the Baldwin room at the Toronto Reference Library; the City of Toronto Culture Division and Archives. For help with finding and using digital images of a considerable number of photographs from the collection of the Canadian Archives of Mental Health, I should like to thank John Court. Some of these photographs have never before been published, and certainly not in this number.

Many thanks are due to Alec Keefer. He has given much valuable time and thought to this project. As a researcher, his skills are formidable, and used with a sense of purpose that leads on with fearless enjoyment to new materials and new syntheses of information. He has also been an indispensible ally and colleague in the production and editing of this work. It is in acknowledgement of his contribution this note is necessary, but hardly adequate as recognition of the vitality and uniqueness of his contribution. And Peter Razgaitis for his attention to detail.

Finally, to the members of the Toronto Branch of Architectural Conservancy of Ontario, and to the members of the Museum of Mental Health Services, thank you all for your patience.

Edna Hudson

PROLOGUE

THE STORY OF THE TORONTO ASYLUM, like that of many institutions and probably more so with psychiatric hospitals, is hidden under layers of experience. Even the overall outline can become clouded when the people describing it use different ways of thinking and different language. When we read the original documents; letters and diaries, annual reports of Government Inspectors and Superintendents and so on, it was not an easy task to understand them. For these pages are of the instant, were not intended for our eyes, and do not strive to tell a conventional story, nor speak to the non-initiated. Lucky for us, that is to a much lessor extent true of plans and elevations prepared by engineers, surveyors and architects whose work of necessity must be reality based. Taken all together the many pasts of an institution are in an animated dialogue with the present. And sometimes heated arguments ensue.

We have taken the documents at their word. The authors existed in a highly competitive environment. They were valued and respected people with no intention to deceive, and we are heirs to their culture. As they wrought so do we enjoy. We communicate these parallels at the outset, in order that we and you can read with fresh understanding. From a foundation that is firm and true, one may construct a social history of the institution that is appropriate to its past context.

Emphasizing the architectural history has greatly helped build the historical ideas, for this topic is given scant attention in the history of asylums. Buildings tell stories, and they do not forget. The architect given a project, necessarily expresses certain values in what he does, it is impossible to design anything 'value-free' — and in the case of habitable buildings, those values are impressed on the public who must use them as well. Similarly, any later modifications must also be made from a value set, and may very well be a re-interpretation in conflict with the original values. All this is demonstrated over and over in any institution with a long history, and is perfectly normal. To focus on architecture to tell the story of the institution is not so usual. This book presents a series of essays that bring together a number of different points of view and an extended discussion of the architecture of the Queen Street asylum.

Our focus is historical, our methods discursive, illustrated and analytic. The resources of historical illustrations, architectural drawings, surveyors maps, photographs and so on have been diligently sought, and we have been able to illustrate our arguments and give resonance to each. The pictures and text work together to create meaning, to enrich understanding.

In fact the meaning given by the illustrations had made a strong bid at times to tell a new story, to require a re-assessment and re-writing of the text.

The first chapter by Dr. Cyril Greenland is a selection from historic materials.

The next is by Dr. Douglas Richardson which sets the cultural context of Toronto in the 1840s and 50s, through analysis of a book on architecture written at the time. This is a culturally broad, pleasant and relaxing read, making an inviting setting for many imaginative forays.

The third chapter is by Pleasance Kaufman Crawford, on the setting of the asylum, the landscaping challenges set and met.

The next two chapters are about the building of the asylum. In chapter four, Alec Keefer describes the political and social context of the time and the influences on Howard as an architect, both before and after his emigration in 1832. Shirley Morriss rounds out the story with more details of Howard's architectural practice and biography.

Chapter six is taken up by Christine Johnston with information on the second superintendent, Joseph Workman and his professional achievements.

The next chapter, by Steven Bell, an exercise in architectural contrast and comparison is a thoughtful consideration of form and its expression of values.

Chapter eight, by Alec Keefer, considers the career of the third superintendent, Dr. Daniel Clark. Especial attention is given to the architectural improvements during his long tenure.

Bill Brown is mainly interested in the Training School for Nurses, founded in 1906 at the asylum, and will fuel reminiscence for many.

The last two chapters lean away from architecture, towards politics and administration. John Court sets out the experiences of the post-Second World War period, when reconstruction was pondered, proposed and enacted. Edna Hudson starts from a factual basis in Howard's 1845 tour of asylums in the US, continues into a discussion on what we have now and why. The dialectic method is very powerful here in defining overarching social causes and their consequences.

Now that the Howard, and the Tully wings are completely gone, the administrative problem has changed. Several of the essayists here are pushing for administrative change, believing that better outcomes for patients will follow. Others take a more reflective stand, wanting chiefly to understand better the nature of the catastrophe.

The possibility of restoration of the historic building is gone forever beyond our reach. No recreation can take its place. Our best efforts to build a memorial have therefore been directed towards this book. We want to give you an accurate understanding of the past, an anchoring in reality. From which study we may know ourselves better.

Most important though, is that the book be enjoyable — only that will make the effort worthwhile. We hope you will find the story absorbing, and worthy of sharing with your friends!

F.W. Micklethwaite (1849-1925)

Frank W. Micklethwaite was born in England, though the family later moved to Ireland. The son of a photographer, Micklethwaite had a chance to learn his profession, possibly as an apprentice, before emigrating to Canada around 1875. After a brief stint as a proof reader for *The Mail* newspaper, Micklethwaite opened his commercial photography studio at his home on Queen Street West in 1878.

For the next 30 years, Micklethwaite operated his studio at various locations around the City, and a seasonal studio at Port Sanfield in the Muskoka Lakes. Micklethwaite's reputation grew and financial stability improved during this period and numerous assignments came his way. Between 1891 and 1898, for example, he was commissioned by the City of Toronto to document a number of public works projects. These photographs, for which Micklethwaite was paid a total of $310, record major reconstruction of the City's water and sewage systems, street grading projects and bridge improvements. In addition, many of his pictures were used to illustrate the annual *City Engineer's Reports.* Respected by his peers, Micklethwaite was asked , in 1893, to participate in the judging of the Second Annual Toronto Camera Club Exhibition. The business produced quality images that document many Toronto landmarks, street views and prominent social gatherings.

Apart from his business interests, Micklethwaite was for many years a member of the Sons of England and the Wilson Masonic Lodge. In failing health towards the end of his life, Micklethwaite increasingly entrusted the operation of the studio to his sons John, Percy and Fred, and it was willed upon his death to Fred.

. ONE .

MADNESS AND THE MEDIA
1840 s - 1990 s

by Cyril Greenland

EVEN BEFORE THE PROVINCIAL LUNATIC ASYLUM received its first patients on 26 January 1850, the press played a lively role in reporting on mental illness and its treatment in Upper Canada. Some of these indelible, but soon forgotten, accounts of scandals and tragedies mark the long and tortuous passage from the goals of the 1840's, to the Queen Street Mental Health Centre of the 1980's and finally to the Centre for Addiction and Mental Health created in 1998.

Our initial plan to publish representative reports gleaned from press from each decade over the past one hundred and fifty years proved impractical for two main reasons. First, examining the micro-film files of the various newspapers was extremely arduous and time consuming. Second, since the press tended to headline negative events such violent deaths and associated calamities, a sampling of news items provided a depressing and grossly unbalanced picture of life in the Asylum. For example, press reports during Dr. Daniel Clark's tenure as Medical Superintendent (1875-1905) were dominated by accounts of Coroner's Inquests into deaths due to suicide. This included a Hospital Bursar who, suffering from depression, drowned himself in Lake Ontario.

Preference was given to articles providing unusual insights into the political and social realities governing the practice of institutional psychiatry in the period under review. The extracts presented here will, it is hoped, provide a vivid account of progress as well as record the suffering of countless patients and their families. Unfortunately, since this was rarely considered newsworthy, stories about the dedication of the professional staff who shared many of the hardships, and were often repaid with harsh criticism, was rarely, if ever, noted by the press. The absence of first hand accounts by patients of life at 999 Queen Street is also regretted.[1]

Although it was common knowledge that the Asylum and later the Ontario hospitals were prime sources of political patronage, this is rarely mentioned in the press. References to this topic were usually muted or presented in coded form. For example, Dr. C. K. Clarke referred to the 'malign influence of politics over psychiatry'[2] but the precise nature of his concerns were never made clear. And since both of the main political parties were involved in these self-serving practices, the M. L. A.'s of the time were reluctant to question the baleful consequences of 'pork barrel' politics.

Rule Britannia

An account of a corner stone laying ceremony was published in the *British Colonist* on Saturday, the 22nd of August, 1846. Its lyrical tone suggests that the decision to construct the new Provincial Asylum, was buttressed by public support and a mood of optimism[4]:

> '...the sun's gladdening beams brightened all around.' Led by the band of the 81st Regiment, the large company slowly made its way out the Hamilton Road to the government military reserve. There, with a silver trowel presented by the building's architect, John G. Howard, Chief Justice John Beverly Robinson ceremoniously spread the mortar to set into place the 'corner stone of the first building in Western Canada for the reception of Insane and Lunatic Persons...' Following an eloquent and heart-felt address by Robinson, the crowd responding with enthusiasm, gave three cheers

for the Chief Justice, the band struck up 'Rule Britannia', and the great gathering dispersed.

Pestilential Conditions at Toronto Lunatic Asylum, c1853

Shortly after his appointment as Medical Superintendent (1853-1875), Dr. Joseph Workman published a damning report on the 'pestilent conditions' in the Provincial Lunatic Asylum. This and his later reports on the baleful effects of chronic over-crowding at the Asylum, symbolize the cycle of optimism followed by disenchantment so characteristic of the history of psychiatry.

After noting that every part of the institution 'abounded with foul air', Dr. Joseph Workman discovered the most enormous cess-pool that perhaps ever existed under a large building. This accumulation of three and one half years of filth was sixty feet in width and from three to five feet deep. The stench from this cess-pool, when first exposed, was so insufferable and overpowering as instantly to sicken several of those who chanced to inhale it. 'Such was the limpid Pieran spring from which the January Grand Muses (Grand Jury) drew their inspiration...no physician having a due regard for the lives and health of his patients, or for his own reputation, could tolerate its continuance.'[5]

During the next winter, Workman directed patients to cut the frozen excrement into blocks and haul it to the garden where it melted in the next thaw.

The wit of Rabelais

This is not the place to discuss the long standing battles,[6] including an action for libel, between Joseph Workman and the editor of the *Globe*, George Brown. But it may be useful to observe that their mutual antipathy spills onto the pages of the Medical Superintendent's annual report for the year 1873 and into the editorial pages of the *Globe* on 12 December 1874. After listing the newspapers supplied gratis to the Asylum, Workman wrote:

> The Liberal publishers of Canada merit the continued gratitude of our people. I wish I could include *The Globe* and *Mail* in the list, but these journals have lunatics enough outside this Asylum to find food for without adding to their number.

Responding to Workman's jibe, the *Globe*'s editor wrote:

> We have heard before of lunatics who thought all the outside world mad, but never before did we see the idea developed in an official report...ghastly attempts at humour...A report is expected to be direct, business-like, concise; and if a man with the wit of Rabelais had to write an account of a year's management of a prison or an asylum the display of it would be an impertinence.

In the same editorial Brown also took exception to Workman's impish account of the discharge of two long-standing patients. Workman's account follows:

> The recovery of the two longest resident females, who were both very well known to you, did not take place recently. Both might have been discharged long ago, had any comfortable home been commendable. One was nearly seventy years of age, and had for years suffered intense mental agony, under the malevolence of an evil spirit, which used very bad language and kept her in terrible bondage. Happily this persecutor at last gave up his naughty tricks, and we had the unspeakable happiness of seeing our good old honest friend go back to her kindred sound in mind and very fat in body.

What shall be done with the Toronto Asylum?

Dr. C. K. Clarke's observations on the future of the Toronto Asylum come from his Annual Report of 1906. The following summary reveals that by 1905, due to overcrowding and neglect, John Howard's Asylum was dilapidated:

> Sixty years ago Toronto Asylum would have been structurally competent to meet the requirements of the situation, and when the building was erected, its location was largely determined by the inhabitants of Toronto, who did not foresee the future growth of their city. The site was then an excellent one, and the surrounding farm and grounds large enough to furnish employment for the patients. At that date the ward population was drawn largely from the agricultural classes.

> In due course the east and west wings were erected and a certain amount of accommodation provided for paying patients. The wards were heated by means of a cumbersome hot-water system, which was thought to be a distinct advantage on the crude methods then generally in vogue. At its very best it would not heat the wards without the addition of many great fires. As years passed, that system was, to a certain extent reorganized and added to, but it is a question if the efficiency was materially increased.

> At the present time, many of the wards are so cold that the patients suffer severely during the winter. This is particularly the case in the wards of the main building, the long corridors of which are at times, too cold to be occupied by delicate patients, whose physical ailments should obtain for them every comfort that a properly heated building will give.

To remedy these defects would cost an immense sum, as it would mean the removal of the mass of piping now in place; the institution of a steam plant in a central station, and the re-piping of the whole building under almost impossible conditions. Whatever faults Toronto Asylum may have, it cannot be said that the contractors scamped their work, and wherever brick walls are to be pierced, or torn down, it is abundantly evident that lime and good bricks were not spared in the construction. If a new heating plant is to be installed, the labour will be Herculean and, if Toronto Asylum is retained, the re-heating must be undertaken at once. It is not humane to expose sick persons, who are nec-essarily prisoners, to the hardships entailed by the ineffi-ciency of this heating system.

If the heating arrangements are open to censure and con-demnation, what shall be said of the plumbing? Its present condition is deplorable, and while it might be an interesting study to one who might wish to compare the sanitation methods of sixty years ago with those of the present, its existence at as advanced a period as 1906 is an anomaly. The closets and bathrooms are a menace to the health of the inmate. Something has been done in the last year to remove a few of the glaring defects, which really constitute the most depressing feature of the Toronto Asylum, but only radical reforms will provide a proper remedy, and these mean the expenditure of a large sum.

...a large Asylum population requires suitable surroundings; plenty of breathing space in a quiet locality, where fresh air and restful conditions generally are obtainable. At Queen Street West, the antithesis of these requirements is the case. Instead of the desirable two or three hundred acres, some twenty-six acres are enclosed within the gaol-like walls; the days and nights are made hideous by electric cars on the one side, and railway traffic passes directly by the south wall, where a freight shunting yard is also located. Queen Street, one of the busiest thoroughfares in the city, is directly to the north. The smoke from the many trains and factories in the neighbourhood pollutes the air. A more undesirable site for the insane could not possibly be selected. It is scarcely possible to conceive that sick people suffering from nervous maladies can be properly treated in a building so situated

Clarke argued that since a great deal of government money had already been spent to build the Asylum, the various options should be considered with great care. At the outset, he recognized that an institution serving an urban population must be close to the city. Next, since the training of medical students is important, the distance from the University must not be unreasonable. Concluding that the thirty-four acre site must be immensely valuable, if sold the money received would pay for the building of a new asylum within reasonable distance from Toronto.

As a result of Clarke's analysis, the government was persuaded to purchase land at Whitby and to build the Ontario Hospital, Whitby with a bed capacity of 1,582. This cottage-style mental hospital, with a large farm, was eventually opened in 1919. A further consequence of Clarke's indictment of the building was that the provincial government was relieved of its responsibility to underwrite improvements. To quote Clarke, the flame was not worth the candle.

Dr C. K. Clarke recommended the building of a Psychiatric Clinic close to the University of Toronto. This, he said, should have an intimate relationship with the Provincial General Hospital but should be under the direct management of the Hospital for the Insane. 'Such a clinic would not interfere with the function of the psychopathic ward in the General Hospital, a ward which deals largely with neurasthenics, rather than insane persons.'[7] The opening of the Whitby Hospital and the Ontario Psychiatric Hospital in 1925, modeled after Kraepelin's Clinic in Munich[8] provides a measure of C. K. Clarke's authority and his influence with the government. But nothing was done to stem or reduce the demand for mental hospital beds in Ontario. Therefore, instead of being sold, 999 Queen Street continued in use.

The great demolition debate

Towards the end of 1975, a public controversy erupted in Toronto concerning the government's proposal to demolish the oldest and only remaining part of the original Provincial Lunatic Asylum and to use the site for a parking lot. Powerful arguments for and against the demolition were presented in letters to the press. Describing the Howard building as 'a forbidding presence', Professor F. H. Lowy, chair of the University of Toronto, Department of Psychiatry, argued that it was 'a visible reminder of a previous era of treatment of the mentally ill from which, thankfully, we have emerged.' In contrast, his colleague Dr. Robert Pos, who opposed the demolition, described the old building as 'an inalienable part of the history of Canadian psychiatry.'[9] A much more personal perspective on the demolition debate was provided by Joan Sutton, a columnist with the Toronto Sun, 17 December 1975.[10]

> So they want to save 999, I wonder if they were ever in it. I was once. I was a volunteer, but it was soon evident to me that the line between those who could leave at night and those who had to stay behind locked doors was a vague one. It was a line composed of chance, genes, luck, money, love, family support. Some of us had those things. Others didn't. Once a group of male and female volunteers organized a dance. While they were dancing, he made small talk. 'How long have you been a patient?' he crooned. The woman

reeled in shock. 'A patient? I'm not a patient. I'm the president of a service club...' No, you couldn't always tell the difference. Sometimes of course you could. There was the ward on the fifth floor where you thanked God each time you visited for the difference.

Patients endangered at Queen Street

Over its long history, Queen Street has weathered many tragic episodes but the nadir was probably reached in the early 1980's. Warnings that Ontario's mental health system was seriously flawed were given by the Committee on Mental Health Services in its 1979 report *Agenda for Action.* But due to the lack of effective Ministerial leadership and action, a potentially dangerous situation was allowed to fester.[11]

Adding insult to injury, in the Spring of 1981 a hiring freeze was ordered by the government. As a result, medical and other professional staff who left Queen Street could not be replaced. In this period, eight psychiatrists and twenty-one other staff had left. In these strained circumstances, one could hardly be surprised to learn that, the death on 23 June 1980 of nineteen-year old Aldo Alvani was attributed to staff shortages. An in-patient at Queen Street, Mr Alvani died after receiving large doses of tranquilizing drugs. This tragedy was compounded by the unexpected deaths of Patricia Ellerton in August and Austin Davis in December, 1981. All three deaths occurred at the weekend, when the hospital was most seriously understaffed. When Austin Davis died, two psychiatrists were caring for about five hundred patients. This desperate situation was duly reported by the Globe & Mail and by the Toronto Star. Both papers were critical of the Ministry of Health and the Star called for an independent inquiry into conditions at the hospital.

On 12 July 1981, the *Globe & Mail* published a report based on a letter addressed to the Hon. Dennis Timbrell, Minister of

Health, by the President and nine current and past members of the executive of Queen Street's medical staff association. Noting that there had been a sixty-six percent increase in the number of staff injuries because 'frustrated patients have lashed out violently to staff.' The report continued:

Psychiatric patients at Ontario's largest mental health centre are endangered by inadequate care resulting from a Government hiring freeze put on the hospital last Spring... Queen Street is being run as a plant recycling emotionally disturbed people: staff as well as patients are being depersonalized because of a lack of involvement in decision-making.

Deaths at Queen Street

The list of Jury recommendations from the inquest into the death of Patricia Ellerton was published in *Phoenix Rising*, (2.4) April 1982. Determining that Ms. Ellerton's death was due to an overdose of Nozinan, a drug used to treat paranoid schizophrenia, the Coroner learned that, at the time of her death, only one physician was on duty to care for six hundred patients.

Since the source of the drugs was unknown, the Coroner's Jury heard evidence of the availability of illicit drugs in the Mall area which was open to the public. Sergeant Roy Teeft, investigating officer for the inquest, reported that while undercover, he received any drugs he asked for through pushers who came into the mall. He said he could have had drugs, alcohol and even sex if he had wanted it and was willing to pay.

Recommendations of the Jury

MALL AREA

1. Additional uniformed security guards to supervise the mall area

2. Passes be issued (with photograph) to ensure only legitimate people make use of the mall.

3. Restrict ingress and egress to one entrance to and from the mall to validate passes.

4. we support the establishment of a liaison group between the security force and Metro Police to monitor mall area for illicit activities.

5. We support the planned installation of surveillance cameras in the hospital wards, we suggest in addition that such cameras be also considered for the mall area.

MEDIUM SECURITY CONCEPT

The jury supports the suggested medium security wing concept as mentioned by Dr. Durost. We would accept that such a concept would result in restrictions being placed on involuntary patients and those requiring special supervision.

INVENTORY OF STOCK DRUGS

The jury accepts that narcotic drugs are closely controlled within the hospital. We would recommend planned periodic checks be made on stock drugs to ensure that individual dispersal equal actual consumption. This would be be carried out under the supervision of a pharmacist. The more widely used drugs could be monitored at regular intervals with no prior notice of the drug to be checked.

HOSPITAL PROCEEDURES

Emergency Practice (Code 99)

We recommend that emergency proceedures be conspicuously posted and reviewed with all staff at intervals.

Reinforce Bed Check.

We recommend a) night lights in rooms; b) set up an hourly checklist and have nurses initial check it.

COMMENDATIONS

The jury commends: 1) the day staff of the Queen Street medical facilities for devotion, interest, and 2) Swed Murtaza, the security guard, for volunteering his testimony to the inquest

1990's detritus of market economics

An OPSEU strike, from 26 February to 30 March 1996, put a great strain on the hospital which continued to care for its population of mostly chronically ill patients. The strike was equally hard on staff. The apprehensive feelings of Marg Gorrie, a clinical nurse specialist, is brilliantly conveyed in her article published in Facts and Arguments section of the *Globe & Mail*, 18 March 1996:[11]

> My twenty years of nursing hasn't prepared me for this. Like most of my fellow pickets, I have never been on strike before. The experience is exciting and sometimes frightening, while managing also to be tedious. I stand on Queen Street West with other nurses, recreation staff, occupational therapy assistants, maintenance workers and housekeeping and kitchen staff wearing a sign urging passers-by to help save the public services. I picket on the evening shift 3 to 11 p.m. twice a week in order to earn my $100-a-week strike pay.
>
> The homeless, the chronically mentally ill, prostitutes and their pimps, and public sector workers: We share the street now, the 1990's detritus of market economics. With the possible exception of the prostitute, our activities are currently depicted by the media as a drain on society. I am now to understand that the assistance I have been providing to persons whose lives are damaged by overwhelming fears, inexplicable aggression and loss of memory is 'fat' which must be cut away.

Epilogue

Because mental illness is inherently tragic, most of the material presented in this chapter reflects an unavoidable sense of sadness. But if nothing else, the history of psychiatry confirms Alexander Pope's belief that 'hope springs eternal in the human breast.' According to many experts, recent advances in understanding brain chemistry and related developments in psychopharmacology herald the golden age of psychiatry. The current mood of optimism, reflected in ambitious plans to re-develop the Queen Street site, provides a fitting topic for our epilogue.

Divestment from the Ontario government had been on and off Queen Street's agenda for several decades. Consequently, the decision to merge with the Clarke Institute of Psychiatry, the Addiction Research Foundation and the Donwood Institute to form the new Centre for Addiction and Mental Health, was no surprise.

While welcoming the merger, the community of people interested in Queen Street's history were troubled. Some of us were deeply concerned because CAMH's Board of Trustees was ominously silent about its responsibility to preserve the artifacts, the history and the site of Upper Canada's first purpose built asylum. However, in recent months, CAMH announced its decision to 'seriously assess the creation of a Centre of Excellence at the Queen Street site as the hub for the Centre's operations.'

The statement continues:

The Queen Street site is the only site that allows the Centre to meet its philosophy of client-centred care and the Ministry of Health and Long Term Care's planning guidelines, and offers efficiencies in both capital and operating costs. The development of the Queen Street site, also provides the Centre an opportunity to play a positive role in the regeneration and redevelopment of the surrounding neighbourhood, transforming the site from its association as a provincial psychiatric asylum to a Centre of Excellence — a full teaching hospital providing clinical treatment, prevention, education and research in the field of addiction and mental health.

The organizations dedicated to preserving Toronto's historic past will, no doubt, welcome the opportunity to become involved in the regeneration and development of the old Garrison common lands. However in contemplating these exciting developments, we should remember that the Provincial Lunatic Asylum in Toronto, opened a hundred and fifty years ago, was in its day a Centre of Excellence and the birthing-place of psychiatry in Upper Canada.

. TWO .

THE ASYLUM
IN CONTEXT

by Douglas Scott Richardson

TORONTO EXPERIENCED AN ASTONISHING EXPANSION from the mid-1840s through the early '50s — reflected in truly great buildings like John George Howard's Asylum — that must have amazed those who had known the community earlier on.[2] Yet the tone of wonderment that one might expect to find appears only occasionally in Victorian publications. Thus, Professor Daniel Wilson writes in 1858 'this capital of Upper Canada has been hewn out of the woods, and cleared out of the swamps, within the memory of living men.'[3] The question that concerns us in the present chapter is essentially this: during the Asylum's construction, and in the following decade or so, what was its urban context, broadly considered, in terms of the cityscape, streetscape, or buildings of note? And, beyond such physical concerns, what was the intellectual climate of the architects who created the public works, the communal monuments?

Newspapers, including those from outside Toronto, were not reluctant to comment on the city's prospects and fine appearance. The Brockville *Statesman* remarks as early as 1845 that 'The improvements in this good City are even much greater than we expected.' It comments on four new churches (including the just-begun Roman Catholic cathedral); finds the university grounds and College Avenue (now University Avenue) and adjacent Cricket Fields 'much improved' and 'really delightful'; notes the striking addition of the west wing and the beautified grounds at Osgoode Hall; and concludes with three new cut-stone bank buildings that 'will prove a great ornament...and are certain indi-

1. Crystal Palace by Sandford Fleming and Collingwood Schreiber.

cations of the rapidly advancing prosperity of the place.'[4] But no guide book gave Toronto its due until after the mid-century.

Given this state, it is curious that no one seems to have commented on the usefulness of a multifaceted overview that appeared in 1858 (though many have used the work). This is *The Hand-Book of Toronto*, which offers informed insight into the local architectural culture in the period, with nice historical distinctions and, now and then, some meaningful perceptions. At the same time it is clear that the intuition of the *Hand-Book*'s anonymous author is sometimes tainted by partisan inattention. Thus, Howard's ASYLUM of 1846-50, the largest and the most humane of many noteworthy buildings in the city at the time, is referred to simply as a charitable institution; its already overcrowded condition is mentioned sympathetically, but its architectural merits are completely overlooked.

The Hand-Book of Toronto was rushed into print early in the autumn of 1858 by one who identified himself (on the title-page) only as 'A MEMBER OF THE PRESS'. The preface (p. [iii]) traces the origin of the book to the summer of 1855, which means that from conception to production the *Hand-Book* took three years, a conventional gestation period for books and elephants.[5] During the spring and summer of 1858 the author anticipated delivery day as much as any gravid elephant: he had his eye on the approaching Provincial Exhibition and the market associated with it. The 'Ex' (as we have come to know it) was to be housed in sensational new quarters, 'a building principally of iron and glass' **(fig. 1)** that was bound to attract attention, by civil engineers Sandford Fleming and Collingwood Schreiber (p. 199). This stood immediately south of the Asylum, between King and Adelaide streets. Obviously emulating Sir Joseph Paxton's mighty juggernaut of a building for the Great Exhibition of the Industry of All Nations at London in 1851, the new Exhibition Building at Toronto — likewise known as the 'CRYSTAL PALACE' — was small and puny by comparison with its namesake, but it was an example of both a novel building type (one for exhibition purposes), and the innovative building technology associated with such exhibition buildings (derived from greenhouses).[6] Clearly the author was fascinated with Toronto's Crystal Palace, which had been constructed speedily, and made arrangements hastily for an image of it to serve as the book's frontispiece. (The building had been completed only a fortnight when the preface to the book was dated, 20 September 1858 [p. iv].) The author records (pp. 199-204) the rapid sequence of the Exhibition Building's materialization from the design competition (announced as late as 13 April 1858 but closing as early as 24 April), through tendering for construction on 22 May, to laying the cornerstone on 15 July, and completion of the building on 5 September 1858.[7] In retrospect, the frontispiece showing the 'Exhibition Building' seems to have served a dual purpose: a graceful compliment to Fleming & Schreiber that was also calculated to enhance sales of the *Hand-Book*.

A statistical summary in the *Hand-Book* (pp. 78-80) allows us to gauge over-all activity in the Toronto building trades in 1858. The population at the most recent census, in 1851, had been 30,775, and was reckoned to have increased 20,000 over the next seven years. The increase in housing was even more striking: from 3212 dwellings of all kinds in 1850 to 7476 in 1857. When John Howard arrived in 1832 he had been the first trained architect here; two dozen years later there were 11 architects. There were as many bankers, and only three times as many bakers (37). Builders were as numerous as butchers (66). The builders were augmented by a small army in related trades: 51 masons, 91 bricklayers, 496 carpenters, 42 plasterers, 84 painters and 82 cabinetmakers (but only 16 plumbers in the era before indoor facilities were common). Blacksmiths, who supplied much architectural hardware, were almost plentiful (96) — but outnumbered by barristers and solicitors (108). The community's physical growth is also suggested by large numbers of engineers (48), civil engineers and surveyors (23), gardeners (61), and machinists (27). Presumably the last group included the foundry workers whose cast-iron building elements had begun to play important roles in construction.[8] Toronto was obviously a city on the rise.

One copy of the *Hand-Book* in particular gives rise to a new view of both this work and the civic ethos it embodies.[9] This volume is inscribed in faded ink on the flyleaf:

William Hay Esq
with
G.P. Ure's
Kind regards

A certain amount is known about Hay, much less about Ure, and almost nothing about their relationship.

The Scots architect William Hay (1818 – 1888) is remembered in Canada primarily for his association with a few buildings that survive here. Trained in Edinburgh in the architectural office of John Henderson, beginning in 1844, he had been retained in 1846 by Gilbert (later Sir George Gilbert) Scott to act as Clerk of the Works on the Anglican Cathedral of St John the Baptist at St John's, Newfoundland. He set sail for the colony in April 1847, and before completing the cathedral's nave in 1850, he had also advised on work in Bermuda. He then returned to Scotland. He seems to have visited Montreal and Chicago with a view to opening an office, but settled in Toronto by 1852. He was very active in Freemasonry, had a 'kindly and genial disposition', and built up a successful practice. In 1862, within two years of his wife's death, he turned over this practice to his recent partner Thomas Gundry (who immediately formed a partnership with Hay's talented apprentice, Henry Langley). Hay went to Nova Scotia (and again to Bermuda), then back to Scotland.[10] In Kingston his Commercial Bank of 1853 (subsequently the Empire Life building) remains, as does Thornton Cliff, a Gothic Revival villa of

2. Yorkville Town Hall
by William Hay.

1855 in Brockville. For the Roman Catholics of Toronto he designed St Michael's College and St Basil's Church (1855-6). He added a Sunday school with a chapel to the Anglican Church of the Holy Trinity in 1856, and designed the nearby house of 1861-2 for its rector, the Rev. Dr Henry Scadding, both of which survive (though the house has had to be trundled across Trinity Square to rescue it from Eaton Centre). Hay's most memorable Toronto building was the polychromatic Yorkville Town Hall of 1859-60 (**fig. 2**), destroyed by fire in 1941, but recorded in original (and beautiful) architectural drawings by Henry Langley.[11]

George P. Ure, also a Scot, has been identified as the anonymous author of *The Hand-Book of Toronto*. He was, as the enigmatic title-page says, 'a member of the press': a reporter on the

(Toronto) *Globe* in the 1850s and a temperance advocate, he was also the founder of the (Montreal) *Family Herald* in 1859. He died in Montreal, 22 August 1860.[12]

The first Archivist of University College, Thomas A. Reed gave a number of his books to the Archives, including Hay's copy of Ure's *Hand-Book*, adding a pencilled note at the bottom of the flyleaf that outlines Hay's career and concludes: 'Descriptions & illustrations in latter part of this book by Wm. Hay.' At first glance one might think that this simply refers to a couple of plates and the texts they illustrate. But likely more is meant (though Reed's basis for saying so is unclear). At the very least Hay seems to have ghosted many — and possibly all — of the architectural descriptions in Ure's book, which are often distinctly architectural (and sometimes rather biased). As some of the same text appeared in Ure's columns in the *Globe*, Hay was evidently helpful to Ure over a period of time. Had they known each other in Scotland as well? Whatever the case, Hay's descriptions of Toronto offer us a good overview of the city at mid-century, and of the architectural context of Howard's Asylum shortly after its construction.

There are three illustrations and a pictorial map in Hay's copy of the *Hand-Book*. We have already seen that the frontispiece (**fig. 1**) shows the building of the moment, the 'Exhibition Building' or Crystal Palace. Both the designers and the contractors are acknowledged in small type: 'Fleming & Schreiber, C.E.'/ 'Smith, Burke & Co., Builders.' (And in the preface, 'Mr. Seymour' is praised 'for the fineness of detail and the exquisite finish' of this wood engraving.)

It seems that Hay's copy of Ure's book was extra-illustrated as two rather larger views on blue paper are not mentioned in the text and do not seem to occur in other copies of the book.[13] The first supplementary illustration, a woodcut (opposite p. 132), reads:

TORONTO GENERAL HOSPITAL.—WILLIAM HAY, ESQ. ARCHITECT.[14]

3. Project for St. Basil's Church and St. Michael's College by William Hay.

The second illustration, a lithograph, is larger and treated as a gatefold illustration (opposite p. 263). This shows a project not later than 1855 for St Basil's Church and St Michael's College — both now part of the University of Toronto campus (**fig. 3**). It is lettered in the plate:

South West Prospect of
SAINT-BASIL'S CHURCH AND COLLEGE OF SAINT MICHAEL
TORONTO.
Wm. Hay Architect.

We will come back to all three illustrations and to an engaging 'Map of the/ CITY OF TORONTO/ Canada West', which is nor-

mally folded at the back of the *Hand-Book* (**fig. 4**). This fine lithograph, measuring just over one foot by two, is almost unknown
even to specialists (in spite of being reproduced in the 1960s), but
is an essential part of our story.[15]

Before dealing with anything architectural, Ure plods
through thirteen chapters (or 'sections') on topics such as climate,
geology, natural history, statistics, education, the press, charities,
and so on. He rarely refers to buildings, except in the most curso-
ry way, not even when the institutions that are housed in these
buildings call for extended comment. Thus, in the section on
'Education', after more than a page on the University of Toronto
and University College, only passing reference is made to the
'extensive buildings at present in progress in the University Park',
and no mention is made of the architects (pp. 106-7). Nor is there
any indication on the map of the university's existence, let alone
these 'buildings' (housing both college and university in one
structure). There is only a single word, 'PARK'. More than four
pages follow the heading 'Trinity College' without a word about
Kivas Tully's building of 1851-2, even though it is a fairly conspicuous feature in the lower left corner of the map, near the
Asylum and the Crystal Palace (**fig. 5**). Yet Toronto was very
unusual at the time — especially for a city of its size — in having
three universities (before federation united them): the University
of Toronto and its teaching arm, University College (counted as
one); St Michael's College, then a separate institution; and Trinity,
also separate at the time. There were no fewer than four sets of
buildings if one includes the various premises occupied by King's
College, forerunner of the University of Toronto, and recently
vacated.[16] Similarly the Normal School's opening, in 1852, is
noted without comment on the building (pp. 115-16); the centrepiece survives as a sort of folly in the quadrangle of Kerr Hall at
Ryerson Polytechnic University. In the section on 'Charities',
when the incorporation of the General Hospital in 1847 is men-

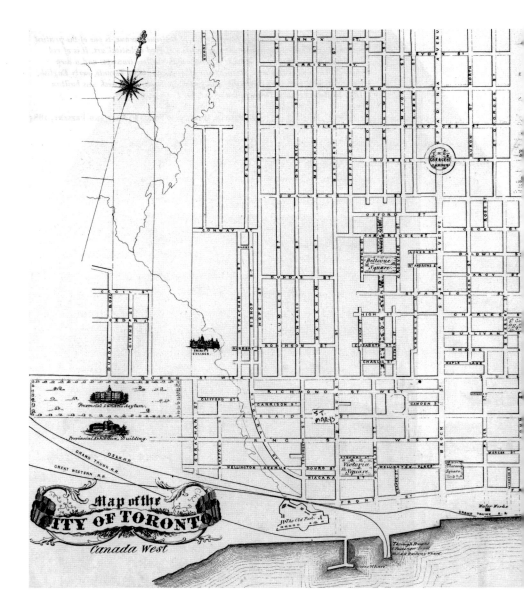

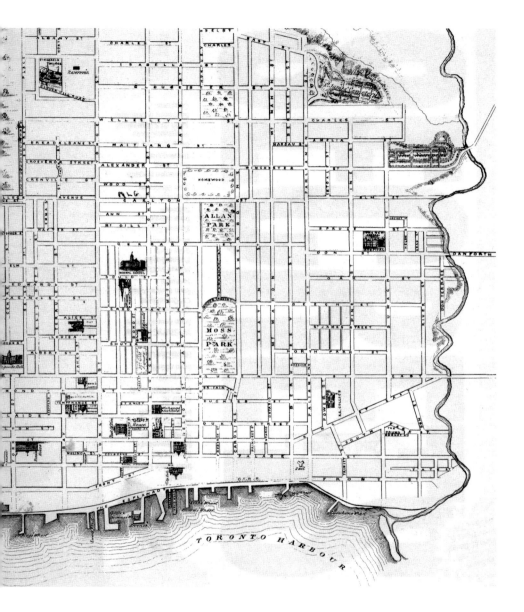

4. Map of the
City of Toronto from Ure's
Hand-Book, 1858.

tioned (pp. 138-9) along with 'more commodious buildings' for the Asylum in 1845, neither the hospital — one of Hay's master-pieces — nor Howard's chef d'oeuvre is discussed, even though both appear on the map, and the latter was then the largest build-ing in British North America. (The hospital, however, will be dis-cussed to excess eventually.) As a last example, the shortcomings of City Council are noted in the long section on 'Municipal Arrangements' (pp. 141-61) without anything about those of Henry Bowyer Lane's second City Hall (1844-5), which is also illustrated on the map. (Lane's building, notorious for its inade-quacies, had to be altered early on.)

The Crystal Palace is really the first building discussed — at length — in the 'Miscellaneous' section, two-thirds of the way through the book (pp. 199-204). The architects, the builders, the 'Founders and Machinists', all are duly mentioned. The same material appears in the *Globe*, Wednesday, 29 September 1858

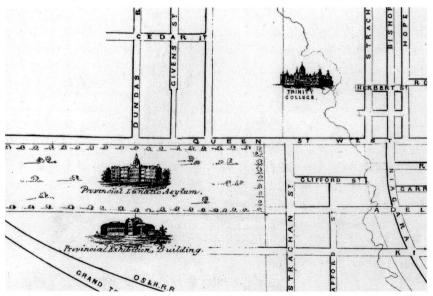

5. Detail of fig. 4, showing Tully's Trinity College (upper right), Howard's Provincial Asylum (centre) and Fleming & Schreiber's Exhibition Building or Crystal Palace (lower).

(which makes one wonder how many descriptions of other buildings in the book had been recycled from Ure's coverage of the laying of cornerstones and the opening of buildings).[17]

It is the long closing section of the *Hand-Book*, 'Public Buildings and Their Locations' (filling pp. 224-70), that finally calls forth much architectural description, part of it in conjunction with 'The very beautiful map which has been engraved [lithographed, in fact] by Mr. [John] Ellis expressly for this work' (p. 224). Ure's preface grabs our attention with the claim (p. iv) that it 'contains a feature never before displayed in any Canadian map, that of giving a microscopic representation of public buildings upon the sites which they respectively occupy'. Some of the smaller buildings are truly miniature on the map. Altogether 25 buildings are shown — usually through an elevation, but sometimes in a perspective view. Many appear on their side, or are even inverted, because the images are turned to make clear the orientation of each building to the street on which it fronts. Virtually all the buildings featured are concentrated in the core area, from Front Street to Gould, between Simcoe and Jarvis (**fig. 6**). Most were then recent, dating from the 1840s and '50s, and an unexpected number are still with us a century and a half on.

A curious feature of the last section of the book is that every major work by Hay (and many a minor one) is mentioned and described, frequently in glowing terms. It also appears that a number of other buildings praised in the text and illustrated on the map are by William Thomas, an architect whose work was very fine, but hardly as progressive in architectural style as Hay's. On the other hand, a number of landmarks shown on the map are not discussed, sometimes not even mentioned, and their architects are therefore overlooked.

The text describing the buildings is arranged so that a very long 'Excursion' is outlined, taking in many of the buildings illustrated on the map. Anyone who has tried to conduct a walking

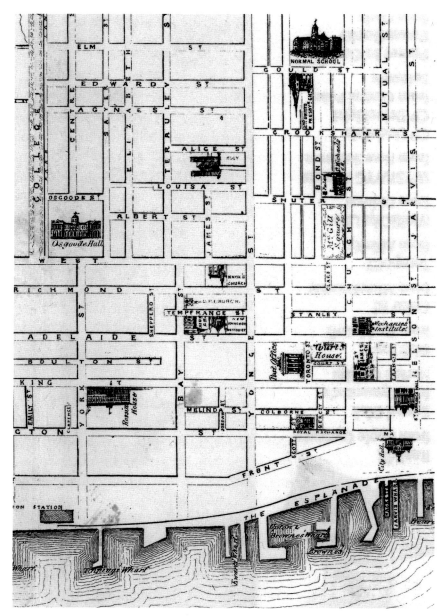

6. Detail of fig. 4,
The core area of Toronto, from Front Street to Elm Street and from College Avenue
(now University Avenue) to Jarvis Street

tour knows that difficulties arise when one plans the route, and some omissions occur naturally. Still, the route taken by the *Hand-Book* is by no means straightforward: in fact, it is very strange indeed. A number of major monuments in the core appear to be avoided. Even odder, perhaps, is the fact that still others *are* discussed without mention of their designers, which seems not so much an oversight as a calculated snub. (In a city as small as Toronto was then, the principal players were all too well known to one another.) What is astonishing is that the architects most frequently slighted one way or another are Cumberland & Storm, then the leading firm of designers in the city, beyond any question. Especially as long detours are made to the city limits only to take in buildings by Hay.

Suppose we join Ure and Hay at the foot of Yonge Street, take a run over the route, and look at a selection of the buildings they describe. (For interest we will also note most of those illustrated on the map and those that survive.) Heading east along Front Street we come to the SECOND CITY HALL (1844-5), between Market and Jarvis streets. Almost vernacular in character, it is described (pp. 225-6), and illustrated, but without a nod to its architect, Henry B. Lane. (Only the central portion survives, housing the Market Gallery of the City of Toronto Archives in the space originally occupied by the Council Chamber.)

The information on the COUNTY JAIL of 1838, on Front at Berkeley, identifies John G. Howard as the architect, and gives it a mixed review as a 'substantial' building (pp. 226-7). Though it is on 'the radial principle' (to facilitate supervision), it is 'totally inadequate for the purpose of classification of the prisoners' and a 'gloomy-looking prison'. (It was demolished in 1887.) Mentioned in passing is the DON JAIL, which was about to be erected to the designs of William Thomas, who is credited with this project.

On King Street East at Trinity Street we come to the small Anglican church of 1843-4 that was already familiarly known as

LITTLE TRINITY. This is scotched as 'an unpretending spurious gothic red brick edifice, built after a design of H.B. Lane'. (After this caustic comment it is striking that Kivas Tully is praised for 'the addition of a gallery and an improved internal arrangement'.) Barely mentioned but faring better — even though similar in style — is its 'very neat parochial SCHOOL HOUSE, erected [in 1848] at the expense of Enoch Turner' (p. 229). Both buildings are extant.

Two long detours follow; the first — far to the east of the Don River, to the race course — is pointless (pp. 229-31). The second, however, takes in two progressive developments still regarded as civic treasures. THE NECROPOLIS (1850), on Winchester Street near the top of Sumach, is described along with its 'very neatly constructed mausoleum' (p. 232). This is a long-demolished mortuary vault, for use in winter ('when the ground is impervious to the mattock'), having nothing to do with the present chapel, superintendent's lodge and gates.[18] Turning to a second burying ground very nearby, ST JAMES' CEMETERY, on Parliament Street beyond Charles Street (part of Wellesley Street today), the *Hand-Book* notes (pp. 226-7) that in 1844-5 John G. Howard was responsible for planning the 'sixty-five acres of rolling ground', described as 'tastefully laid out'. (This sounds like what used to be called a Tom Swifty.) The 'receiving vault' here has been replaced by a distinguished building that was already under discussion: Cumberland & Storm's picturesque and extraordinary Chapel of St James the Less (which incorporates a croft-like mortuary in the basement).[19] The plan of the Necropolis is shown on the folding map, as is that of St James' Cemetery; the second was, and is, more picturesque than the first, but both exemplify the early Victorian concern to achieve utility and beauty through sanitary reform.

After retracing our steps down Sumach Street, we come to 'the new general hospital' on Don (now Gerrard) Street, already known as TORONTO GENERAL HOSPITAL (**fig. 7**). This is one of the most detailed accounts given by the *Hand-Book* (pp. 232-4), and is another of the buildings illustrated on the map. Architects often provided the press with descriptions of their work then — as they still do. TGH, built in 1853-6, was described as both 'a hollow square' and 'a mammoth figure E' in plan, although it was of no great size: at 170 by 120 feet, it would fit into most college quadrangles with room to spare. The description proceeds room by room and foot by foot, with attention to what architects used to call the 'planning requirements' and might now identify as the 'building programme'. This discussion, which could have come only from the architect himself, is overblown, describing the hospital as 'A stately building of the old English domestic style' with 'majestic towers'; at best it looked like a diminutive version of an Elizabethan manor house. The entrance hall is spacious, the full-length corridor is majestic, and the 22-foot-wide stairs are ample (all with a view to ease of circulation, no doubt), while the view from the central tower (about 100 feet high) is 'most magnificent' — as if many patients or visitors were likely to see this in the absence of an elevator. (Elisha Graves Otis had only just invented a practical safety elevator in 1853, shown it at the Crystal Palace Exposition in New York in 1854, and installed one in New York's Haughwout Building in 1857). But otherwise TGH must have been considered state-of-the-art construction technically. (It survived until 1921, partly on that account perhaps.) There were twelve baths and twenty-seven water-closets. Each tower was topped by a steeply pitched mansard roof, and the upper part of the towers at the front corners held water tanks.

> In each corridor there were two hydrants, with hose and the necessary apparatus for protection against fire. Considerable attention has been paid to the ventilation of the entire building....

There was also a system of hot-water and hot-air heating. Such attention to circulation, sanitation, fire protection, venti-

TORONTO GENERAL HOSPITAL.—WILLIAM HAY, ESQ. ARCHITECT.

7. Toronto General Hospital by Willian Hay.

lation and heating was singular at the time. (Comparable concerns were expressed in the competition for the Parliament Buildings at Ottawa, held in 1859.) Curiously, in spite of so lengthy a description and a reference to 'the plan devised by the Architect', Hay is not mentioned.[20] One imagines that this was simply a slip of some kind. In Hay's own copy of the *Hand-Book* the illustration of the hospital opposite the text, proclaiming Hay's authorship in block letters, corrects the omission.

The tour continues down Sumach Street to Queen Street, then jogs west to Power Street to visit OLD ST PAUL'S ROMAN CATHOLIC CHURCH (1822, demolished), which is 'plain...with nothing remarkable in its appearance...but it is one of the antiquities of the place' (p. 234).

The adjacent building, however, was another matter: the HOUSE OF PROVIDENCE was begun by William Hay in 1855-8, and completed by Joseph Connolly in 1880-2. (It was demolished in the 1960s.) A combined orphanage, temporary refuge for immigrants, and home for the aged, quite as large as the general hospital, it was in much the same hybrid manner: mansard-roofed but with Gothic Revival detailing. This is given a very extended entry (pp. 234-6). Its H-shaped plan 'broken up by various projections, both for convenience and effect', its stylish 'French roofs', 'clusters of chimney stacks' and complex rooflines, all give 'considerable variety' and boldness. The interior is reviewed meticulously, especially the chapel (with traceried windows and open timber roof). This time Hay *is* mentioned.

From here the excursion moves west along Queen Street to George Street, and south to Duke (now renamed Adelaide) Street, to see the BANK OF UPPER CANADA, which is still well worth a detour. With an historian's flair for distinctions based on chronology the author refers to this (p. 237) as already the 'oldest banking institution in Toronto,...occupying the oldest bank building in the City'. This 'substantial structure of cut stone', built in 1825-7, is now the earliest purpose-built bank surviving in Canada ('Substantial' seems to have been a favourite adjective of the writer.) The author has an eye on the roots of the architectural profession in attributing the building to a capable amateur:

> The main body of the edifice is...said to have been designed by the late Hon. Dr. [William Warren] Baldwin at a remote date, ere yet the little town boasted of Architects 'cunning in their craft.'

The transformation of Toronto's built form could not have taken place, however, had it not been for John Howard, who arrived in 1832, and other trained architects following him over the course of a quarter-century. The proof is in this bank, at first a good-looking but vernacular building that was given real presence when Howard added a Roman Doric portico of sandstone columns — and cast-iron columns to match in the banking hall — in 1843, followed by graceful wrought- and cast-iron railings around the porch roof in 1846. Yet neither Howard nor his porch is mentioned; and if the writer gives with one hand, he immediately takes something back with the other. He sneers at 'the addition of a wing of white brick, built as uniformly as the nature of the material would permit, yet giving it [the complex] a one[-]sided heterogeneous look'.[21] The addition, made in 1851, has been attributed to Cumberland & Ridout on the basis of the well-known associations between the Bank of Upper Canada's Cashier, Thomas Gibbs Ridout, and the architects Fred Cumberland and Thomas Ridout the younger: Ridout's son and namesake was Cumberland's first partner, the elder Ridout and Cumberland were married to sisters, and the Cumberlands' residence at this point was opposite the bank (in which the Ridouts lived).[22]

Another long detour follows, north up George Street to Gerrard Street, one block west on Gerrard, and then south, on Jarvis Street, noting 'good houses' of the well-to-do (pp. 236-8).

The high point is the philanthropy of George W. Allan of MOSS PARK and the extension of Pembroke Street as a carriage drive between Moss Park (originally the home of his father, William Allan) and Homewood (built for George W. Allan). This drive passed through the ten-acre plot known as Allan Park, with eight large house-lots surrounding a botanical garden of five acres, in a 'circus'. It was the origin of the Horticultural Gardens — now known as ALLAN GARDENS — begun in 1855 by the landscape gardener Edwin Taylor, to which Hay would contribute a large pavilion and a gardener's lodge.

Had the author chosen to do so he might have linked this discussion to another striking feature of the folding map: 'Moss Park', 'Allan Park', and 'Homewood' are not only the largest residential plots identified on the map, but the convention of repeated shrubs is used to show that they are planted with comely trees and gardens (**fig. 4**). Also planted, and shown as such, are the large acreage around the Lunatic Asylum (described in Chapter III by Pleasance Crawford), the cemeteries, the university park, and the grounds around the old Parliament Buildings and old Upper Canada College — not one of which is actually described as an ornamental landscape. In addition to the Allan Park complex, half a dozen residential squares shown on the map recall the great British tradition of the planted proprietary square. Two are worth commenting on particularly: Spadina Crescent (identified as 'Crescent Garden' on the map), which was intended as the circular focus of a beautiful housing development (until acquired for old Knox College in 1873); and McGill Square, a tree-lined green space extending between Bond and Church streets from Queen to Shuter, surrounded by town houses except at the north end, which provided a dignified setting for the long flank of St Michael's Cathedral (until the square was sold to Metropolitan Methodist Church in 1870).[23] Bellevue Square did not arise, and St George's Square (in front of the Church of St George the Martyr) was the name given to today's Grange Park. Only Clarence and Victoria evolved as residential squares, unfortunately both compromised now by warehouses and other commercial buildings.

Turning west on King Street, we pause to admire (as we still can) ST LAWRENCE HALL (1849-50), which is shown on the map, and rates as much space in the text (pp. 238-40) as Hay's TGH or House of Providence. The architect of the elegant building — 'decidedly one of the ornaments of the City' — is roundly applauded for this and other works:

> This pile of buildings, so much admired for the harmony of its proportions, was erected on the site of the old City Hall from the designs and under the superintendence of William Thomas[,] Architect, whose high professional talent and correct taste have tended greatly to the embellishment and improvement of this fine City.

This account, uncharacteristically generous and detailed, was described by Eric Arthur as 'very scholarly'.[24] It, too, must have been drafted by an architect: Hay, or Thomas himself?

In accounts of Hay and Thomas in the *Dictionary of Canadian Biography* neither Frederick Armstrong nor Neil Einarson refers to relations between the two architects. Yet one wonders if a friendship may help to explain the high opinion of Thomas's work, some of which was beginning to seem old-fashioned at this date. (Perhaps the 'milk of human kindness' was at work, for Thomas was known to be ailing; he died of diabetes just two years later.)

F.W. Cumberland's output draws almost as much attention as Hay's: the reason is simply that Cumberland had so many significant commissions during the 1850s. A few of these are illustrated in the microscopic views on the map, but otherwise Fred Cumberland and his partners — Thomas Ridout and William G. Storm in succession — are not only given short shrift: they are hardly mentioned. Descriptions of their work are terse, grudging, and even negative in vein, with architectural criticism of a specialized sort not expected from a layman. For example, the author now moves west along King Street and turns north on Church Street, describing (and illustrating on the map) ST JAMES' CATHEDRAL (1850-3). Appreciative at first, he credits this 'massive structure' in 'early English style of the middle of the 13th century' to Cumberland. Here the selection of the word *structure* conveys something of the tectonic quality of the building — as much a work of forceful engineering as of decorative architecture — and the fact that it does indeed seem *massive* in spite of all its vertical elements is owing largely to Cumberland's exceptional feeling for horizontal, solid, and heavy forms. The text goes on to decry the 'large flank porches, giving the effect externally of low transepts, an effect which it could have been wished were realized in its internal arrangement.' This sophisticated criticism must have come from Hay, who was drawing a comparison, in effect, with G.G. Scott's design for the cathedral in Newfoundland, which Hay had supervised and which called for full transepts (not built, however, until decades later). But Hay arrived in Toronto too late to witness Cumberland's frustrated attempts to build a large cruciform church with transepts as high as the nave and complemented by their own aisles in traditional British fashion. Though some of the neomedieval detailing is admired, and the open timber roof is even said to be 'very florid and elegant', in the end exception is taken to the then-incomplete tower and the unorthodox orientation of the building with its sanctuary to the north (pp. 240-1).[25]

At the same time (1851) the same firm produced ST JAMES' PAROCHIAL SCHOOL, fronting on Church Street just behind the cathedral (**fig. 8**).[26] 'It is an ornament to the street, but is somewhat disfigured by a very disproportionate bell tower, of certainly an antediluvian style.' This remark may be Ure's, as Hay would

8. St. James' Parochial School by Cumberland & Ridout, (right) with the Mechanics' Institute by Cumberland & Storm, (in the background).

have known that antediluvian was about the highest term of praise that an Anglican architect could aspire to in the imitative phase of ecclesiastical design at the mid-century.

Still on Church Street, the MECHANICS' INSTITUTE of 1853-61 (demolished in 1949) is illustrated and credited to Cumberland.[27] (This is also visible in **fig. 8.**) Little attempt is made to qualify the eclectic design in a rather long description (pp. 242-3), but the author suggests that:

> A combination of the florid, or decorative, with the substantial, seems to have been the aim of the architect, and in carrying out his design he has given the building an imposing and stately appearance.

This is not a bad summation of most of the firm's work, and the kindest thing said about it in Ure's book.

The excursion moves west on Adelaide Street to the YORK COUNTY COURT HOUSE of 1851-3 (p. 243). Cumberland (alone) is recognized once more.[28] But his work is criticized:

> This is a massive and substantial Roman Doric building executed with an apparent economy which is scarcely in keeping with the decorated style of public buildings generally adopted in the City.

The central portion of this majestic building still stands — in a modern classical vein suggesting that Cumberland was inspired by the great Prussian architect, Friedrich Schinkel — but the wings have been transfigured beyond recognition. The court house is also criticized for being crowded, and having 'neither desks nor seats...for the Daily Press', which this time is obviously the complaint of Ure, the reporter.

Turning south on Toronto Street, we come to the SEVENTH POST OFFICE, by the same firm in the same years (1851-3). Although altered needlessly in exterior details, and utterly changed internally, it stands. Illustrated on the map, it is praised as 'A very fine specimen of Grecian architecture', and rather minutely described for efficient arrangement rather than for form (pp. 242-3).[29]

The MASONIC HALL of 1857-8 stood on Toronto Street (until 1964), immediately north of the post office, and is also discussed at length (pp. 245-8). The cast-iron columns of its storefronts, its large sheets of plate glass in iron sashes, and its iron shutters are all noted. The architect, William Kauffmann, is quoted as identifying it with 'the Modern Munich' in style — presumably meaning that it reflects the Italian Renaissance manner of Friedrich von Gärtner, and the round-arched style (*Rundbogenstil*) of Kauffmann's German origins. Rationalism is inherent in the description: 'we are told that he purposely avoided all heavy projections on the front to avoid the effects of heavy rain or frost.' But in the interior more attention is paid to Masonic iconography and to comparatively minor fittings: 'a gorgeous *Corona-lucis*' (i.e. the hanging light fixture) in St Andrew's Lodge is given nearly half a page of description, and the furniture in the chapter room is also described at length. Both were designed by Hay, not Kauffmann.[30]

The HOME DISTRICT (or YORK COUNTY) REGISTRY OFFICE (**fig. 9**) that used to stand on Toronto Street, opposite the Masonic Hall, is dismissed curtly in half a sentence as a 'small dull-looking, fireproof building' (p. 248). Yet this design of 1848-9 by Cumberland — who is unnamed — was a notable and innovative structure of incombustible materials (with doors, window sashes, and shutters, all of iron), and entirely brick-vaulted. The round-arched external elements reflected the constructional character internally. The façade was kept simple to minimize the cost, yet was a scheme capable of embellishment: the building was the prototype for registry offices — often rather more ornamental — built all over the province beginning a decade later.[31]

Continuing southward by a round-about route, the tour comes

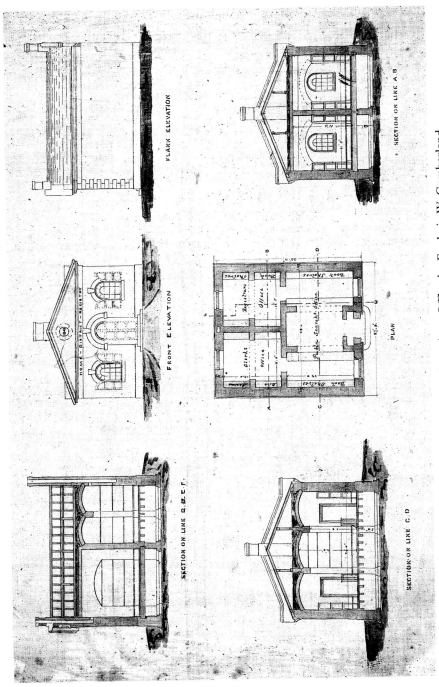

FLANK ELEVATION

FRONT ELEVATION

HOME · DISTRICT · REGISTRY

SECTION ON LINE A B

PLAN

SECTION ON LINE G. H. E. F.

SECTION ON LINE C. D

9. Home District (or York County) Registry Office by Frederic W. Cumberland.

to the TORONTO EXCHANGE of 1854-6 (also illustrated on the map) at Wellington street. This was a choice three-storey office block, an early example of the type, but demolished in 1941. Although given a lengthy description (pp. 249-51) and allowed to be a 'handsome new building' (with neoclassical detail and interesting plan), it is described in the flattest language. Only the 'Exchange' proper — a room '50 feet by 30, of an oval form, by a height of about 40 ft., and lighted by a circular ornamental glass dome' — elicits enthusiasm for the work of its architect, James Grand, who is unnamed.

Having 'nearly reached the point from which we started', the author proposes to walk north up Yonge Street, and begins by admiring the beauty of William Thomas's ROSS, MITCHELL BUILD-ING of 1856 **(fig. 10)**, which stood on the corner of Colborne Street (pp. 251-2):

10. Ross, Mitchell Building by William Thomas (at the left side).

He [Thomas] has proved that it is possible to have much that is graceful and elegant, and at the same time not out of character, in a commercial building. The [stone] front on Yonge Street is very imposing, thirty-six feet in width and four storeys high,...of good colour, and very durable. The style is Italian, with arched windows, the keystones being enriched with ornaments symbolical of Commerce....

Heightening the effect were 'large squares of beautiful English plate glass' — not yet available from Canadian manufacturers — while the interior was 'admirably adapted, in its arrangement, for the purpose designed' (namely wholesale dry goods). 'The establishment is altogether the most handsome and complete structure of the kind which we have in the City', reflecting 'the greatest credit upon the owners, architect and builders'. So imposing and reliable in appearance was this 'model warehouse' that subsequently it served the Bank of Upper Canada, and then became the first head office of the Bank of Commerce.[32]

A detour ensues, west on Adelaide Street, north on Bay and east on Queen, to take in a spate of churches by Thomas (and others), illustrated on the map, and favourably reviewed — if identified as his — and since demolished. First is ZION CHAPEL (1855-6), on Adelaide at Bay, in Thomas's characteristic mix of white brick with Ohio stone dressings, and in 'Lombard style'(pp. 252-3). The NEW CONNEXION METHODIST CHURCH (1846) on Temperance Street, by the same architect (unnamed this time), is condemned as 'A plain structure in the spurious Gothic style' (p. 253). BAY STREET UNITED PRESBYTERIAN CHURCH (1848), between Temperance and Richmond Street, has 'highly ornamental' detail, and old KNOX'S PRESBYTERIAN CHURCH (1847), around the corner on Queen just west of Yonge, is 'handsome'(pp. 254-55). COOKE'S IRISH FREE PRESBYTERIAN CHURCH (1857), 'plain but substantial', is thought worth a detour even though it lies blocks in the opposite direction, at Mutual and Queen (pp. 255-6).

Returning to Yonge Street we are directed — for no particular reason — to another architect's work, Joseph Sheard's ALICE STREET PRIMITIVE METHODIST CHAPEL of 1854 (pp. 256-7), on the site of the Eaton Centre. (It was early turned to commercial use.)

The account of the surviving CHURCH OF THE HOLY TRINITY (1846-7) that follows (pp. 257-8) does not mention its architect, Henry B. Lane, probably because this early local example of the Gothic Revival is considered 'debased'. (It, too, is illustrated on the map.) What is featured instead is an expensive 'stained glass window, designed by Mr. Hay, architect, and executed by Ballantyne of Edinburgh'. (Note the Scots connection once more.) While this window — 'representing life-sized figures of the four Evangelists, under ornamental canopies' — is truly exceptional in the Toronto context of the day (because of its architectural character, its monumental simplicity, and its extensive fields of vibrant colour), the description strikes one almost as a case of the tail wagging the dog. Longer still is the account of the attached PAROCHIAL SCHOOLS, with an open timber roof, another 'neat *corona lucis*', early and 'very good stained glass' by the celebrated local artist in glass, Joseph McCausland (not named) and his house-painting partner (briefly) — who is named — '[William] Bulloch of Toronto', and so on. Significantly, it concludes: '...Mr. Hay furnishing the plans, [he] superintended the construction gratuitously.'[33]

Further north on Yonge we reach Gould Street. We have had too much when Hay is named approvingly as architect of the UNITED PRESBYTERIAN CHURCH (1855-6) that used to stand at the intersection of Gould and Victoria street. In Early English style with 'simple but correct' details, it is dubiously evaluated (and seems vastly over-rated) as 'the chastest architectural edifice in the City' (p. 259).

At this point (pp. 259-63) four pages are lavished on the NORMAL SCHOOL, which is illustrated on the map. It is inescapable not only because it is situated on Gould opposite the last church, but also because of its essential role in the educational system. (Scots almost always evince a lively interest in education.) The account is virtually preoccupied, however, with the corner-stone ceremony and the arrangement of stuffed birds in the museum! Quoting the inscription on the cornerstone is the only way that the architects, Cumberland & Ridout, are mentioned. Nothing but the Roman Doric centrepiece of this focal monument of 1851-2 survives.

Up Yonge Street, past Wellesley Street, we turn west on Clover Hill Road (now St Joseph Street) to visit ST BASIL'S CHURCH AND ST MICHAEL'S COLLEGE (both standing). Hay receives star billing once again (pp. 263-4). It is here that Hay inserted the folded bird's-eye view (fig. 3) — the source of the illustration on the map — in his extra-illustrated copy of the *Hand-Book*. The two buildings are described as if nearly completed in accordance with this early project for a college almost wrapped around a quadrangle. But only the middle of the chapel (without its tower and spire) and the north wing of the college (without a cloister) were constructed in 1855-6.[34] The long and more-or-less laudatory account mentions the architect by name, praises the site, the plan, the 'severe' Early English style, the chapel's open timber roof (now concealed by plaster 'vaults'), and the 'very pleasing and picturesque' effect of the intended complex.

Having gone as far as Bloor Street, 'the northern City limits', the writer turns and passes through the portion of the university grounds we still call Queen's Park, tearing down the length of College Avenue (now University Avenue). His haste and prejudice begin to be more apparent (pp. 265-6). He barely glances at the 'imposing form' of 'the new university buildings' because 'They will not be completed for some time'— a flimsy pretext, as the main range was just being finished, and the Governor General would lay the top-stone on 4 October 1858, exactly two weeks

11. Rossin House by William Kauffmann.

after Ure dated the preface to his book. UNIVERSITY COLLEGE, the teaching arm of the University of Toronto (whose administration it also housed for many years) was constructed in an eclectic version of 'Norman' style and on a grand scale beginning in 1856. Opening in 1859, it was arguably the most important architectural commission of the decade, in the city or the province, and remains a national treasure.[35] Yet it is given the briefest possible description. It is also put down when its innovative Chemistry Laboratory is snidely likened to 'a faithful copy of an old Glass and Bottle Works'. Furthermore, Cumberland & Storm's credit is buried elsewhere, in the description of their Royal Magnetical Observatory (of 1854-5), which follows (p. 266).

At the south end of the College Avenue — today's University Avenue arose then at Queen Street — is OSGOODE HALL, which rates a view on the map (one that is already outdated), but is dismissed in two sentences, using the same formula with even less comment: 'This building is at present undergoing extensive alterations' (p. 266). Thankfully we can confirm with our own eyes today that in 1856-60 the whole central portion was being rebuilt magnificently by Cumberland & Storm (who are unnamed). Admittedly construction work on this plummy commission had been in progress only a year when the *Hand-Book* went to press, yet it is hard to believe that any Toronto architect of the day would be unaware of the noble law library and attractive high courts grouped around the atrium under a square dome of colourful glass. In any case, Cumberland & Storm settled Ure's hash by exhibiting stunning, large watercolour renderings of these and other works at the 1858 Provincial Exhibition.[36]

Southward by York Street (on the axis of Osgoode Hall) we reach the ROSSIN HOUSE (**fig.11**) at King and York streets, William Kauffmann's grand Italian palazzo of 1855-7. It, too, is illustrated on the map, and the architect is named in a decent account of 'Our largest and most handsome Hotel'. The cast-iron and plate-glass

12. Church of St. John the Evangelist by William Hay.

fronts with marble sills are mentioned, the pressed-brick upper storeys with stone dressings, the gas lighting in all 252 rooms, with steam heating in the principal chambers (pp. 266-7).[37] Sadly, however, this five-storey palace hotel, with a total frontage of 355 feet, was demolished for the construction of the Royal Trust Tower in the Toronto-Dominion Centre.

Hay has virtually the last word (or words). Various hands were involved in the old Parliament Buildings on Front Street and they are mentioned. But dominating the account (pp. 267-9) are the additions by Hay, including new galleries in the old Legislative Assembly Room, a library for 30,000 books and a reading room, offices for the Executive Council, and 'a new fire proof building for the PROVINCIAL REGISTRY OFFICE' — described in such a way as to shame Cumberland's County Registry Office, it would appear.

The 'NEW WOODEN CHURCH' (**fig. 12**) on Portland Street at Victoria Square —'a little further west', the author says with some understatement — follows (p. 269). This is the original Anglican Church of St John the Evangelist, or Garrison Church, of 1857-8, a frame building clad in board and batten that lasted into the twentieth century.[38] One may agree that:

> This is a very picturesque and Church-like edifice, and deserving of notice for its severe simplicity yet elegance of structure and design, and its remarkable cheapness.

It was, in fact, an example of a peculiarly North American type of church in which rational gothic principles were applied to wood construction.[39] But it comes as no surprise that 'Mr. William Hay was the Architect.'

With the reconstruction of St Mary's Roman Catholic Church nearby on Bathurst Street, including a school and priest's house by Hay (demolished), the account is not so much rounded off as it is abruptly terminated (pp. 269-70). Fort York, a conspicuous feature of the waterfront, is not mentioned, although 'The Old Fort' is shown in plan on the map (and is still unique for its collection of seven of Toronto's eight oldest buildings, all from the 1810s). Instead the author leaves the reader wandering aimlessly in the already industrial area of Adelaide and Niagara Streets, not far from the Ex (without mentioning the fact). He throws in a 'Conclusion — Arts and Manufactures' (pp. 270-2), which is inconclusive, and confesses to having 'more than exceeded my space'. Ending abruptly, he seems to have run out of time — even before he ran out of steam — if he wanted his book in print to sell at the fall fair.

Hay's contributions to Ure's *Hand-Book* certainly informed and enlivened it. They brought expertise and a certain amount of latent passion to the discussion of Toronto architecture. But the spleen they also reveal would be surprising if we did not allow for several things: the frankness of the press at the time; differences in architectural philosophy; the professional rivalry that must have existed in the 1850s when Cumberland & Storm obtained a lopsided amount of all government work as well as other choice commissions; Hay's dedication to the doctrinaire Gothic Revival as against Cumberland & Storm's thoughtful eclecticism; and finally what may well have been simple personal antipathy.

If Ure's *Hand-Book* was eccentric in plan, much too long, quirky as an architectural escort, and tied to the seasonal Provincial Exhibition, it demonstrated a need nevertheless, and it inspired others. It was followed two years later by a short and charming tourist guide, *The City of Toronto: Illustrated by Oil-Colour Views taken from Photographs* — a work of such rarity that one suspects its fate was either to be carried off by visitors, or to be cannibalized on the spot for its coloured views. Once again the author is unidentified: whoever it is has a good eye, an artistic sensibility, a sure hand, and enough detachment to provide a measured overview that is matchless in the period:

Although not a picturesque city, Toronto is most agreeably situated. The handsome bay...gives it, as a lake port, great commercial advantages, besides adding to the general appearance....The view from the western entrance to the harbour and from the island is varied and striking. The spires and cupolas of its public buildings afford a most agreeable diversity to the distant outline of the city, and mark it as a place of wealth and enterprise. From the cupola of the St. Lawrence Hall at the south, and from that of the Educational Department [i.e. the Normal School] and the new University at the north, the view is both extensive and animating. The long lines of houses, and the rectangular blocks of buildings, intersected by streets running towards the four cardinal points of the compass, with here and there a handsome church or an elegant edifice, strike the stranger with an agreeable surprise.[40]

The book is very short and to the point, with an even-handed treatment of the foremost sights, approached in a rational method. 'In order to take a rapid glance at the chief objects of interest', the writer simply strides the two principal streets: originally King Street, but increasingly Yonge Street. Basically he looks only at buildings on one or other of the two streets — a strategy that suffices. (It resembles, curiously, the principle of the architectural section, taken longitudinally and horizontally.) Following this he offers a gazetteer listing all the notable landmarks. Descriptions name the designer more often than not, and are historical, informative, and dispassionate.

The long note on the Asylum is particularly interesting, describing the building, the character of its site, its location relative to City Hall, the materials used, and finally (in Howard's own words, directly quoted) the main features, pragmatic and aesthetic. As compared with Hay's predominantly visual and stylistic approach, Howard strikes us as modern in his concern for the utilitarian *and* the symbolic programme. Howard speaks to the public weal, but in the last analysis he is also user-oriented. The patients are classified in six ways. Details about 'day rooms' for socializing the patients, and the staggered floor plans — bringing as much light and air as possible into the building while facilitating circulation and fire control — are not presented here.[41] But Howard speaks of the semicircular verandahs, rounding off the geometric *parti* of this megastructure: iron bars 'prevent accidents', yet allow patients fresh air even in poor weather. 'The centre building is surmounted by a lofty dome covered with tin (which can be seen for 30 miles on the lake)', not just to serve as a landmark but to hold an iron reservoir containing 11,000 gallons of water that supplies running water to the whole building.

At this date Howard's description of a gigantic porch of cut stone in the Grecian Ionic order is still quoted, though it never materialized. He clung, as American contemporaries did, to the conviction that public architecture of the highest quality promotes higher public standards of conduct: 'What is the use of the *marble palace*? what the value of the fluted column and gorgeous capital?', asked an orator in Philadelphia on the completion, in 1847, of Girard College. The answer was that transcendent buildings effect change in us, transforming us into 'living temples of moral truth'.[42] It is tempting to interpret one detail of Howard's unrealized portico as speaking eloquently nonetheless to our age — so rich in knowledge and resources, so impoverished in compassion. The royal arms, carved in relief in the pediment, signify the benign and philanthropic support of a caring provincial government with the support of a responsible electorate.

. THREE .

SUBJECT TO CHANGE: ASYLUM LANDSCAPE

by Pleasance Kaufman Crawford

IN MAY 1845, AFTER CONSIDERABLE DELAY, the British Ordnance Department granted for the Provincial Lunatic Asylum a 50-acre (20.2-hectare) rectangle in the northern part of the Military Reserve. The grant was more strategic than munificent. The site was small — half the size of a Toronto park lot and a third to a quarter the size of a typical farm lot — and soon constrained by the requirements of military officers, railway executives, provincial and municipal officials, manufacturers, and developers. From the beginning, the asylum and its landscape have been subject to change brought about by natural forces and human factors.

The Natural Environment

The asylum site had been a Mississauga 'Reserve for Camping and Council purposes.'[1] In 1818, like more than half of the area west of the town and south of today's Queen Street, it was largely covered with young trees and scrub. Among the scattered clearings, however, was one southwest of the present-day intersection of Ossington and Queen.[2] By 1835, much of the uncleared area on the Military Reserve or Garrison Common to the south consisted 'chiefly of young timber[:] Poplar, Hemlock, Maple, Oak, and a few Pines' — the 'large Timber' suitable for ship-building having been 'cut down during the late War.'[3] The asylum site itself, although 'once a black ash swamp', had been at least partially cleared.[4] Surveying it in 1845, John Howard found a toll house, garden, and sheds near the intersection.[5]

By mid-1846 only stumps remained on the property and the

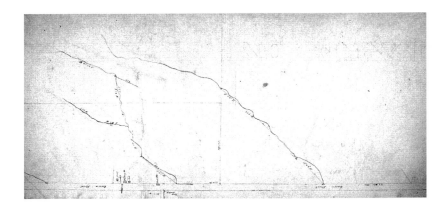

1. Plan of asylum grounds.
Drawn by J.G. Howard, May 1845 [?], detail.
Toronto Reference Library, Howard Collection, L 27, Acc. 945

Commissioners in charge of construction paid ten pounds for removal.[6] Two summers later when Augustus Köllner drew the scene 'from nature,' the area surrounding the building-in-progress was devoid of trees or stumps, although some woods obscured the southern horizon.[7] Early photographs of the completed structure show no nearby woods; yet if left uncultivated and unmown, the ground was apparently quick to produce second growth. In 1879, patients had to cut down 'superabundant' trees before planting crops on the former Crystal Palace grounds immediately to the south.[8]

Garrison Creek lay entirely east of the asylum land. On and near that land, however, John Howard observed 'several small & never failing creeks' but none 'sufficiently high to supply the Tank in the Dome.'[9] The largest of these, later called Asylum Creek, rose north of today's Queen Street and flowed (between banks Howard described as 'a little swampy') across the western portion of the site — where it was later channelized and ultimately buried — and thence into Garrison Creek northwest of the old fort. A smaller creek entered from just west of today's Ossington

Avenue, 'meander[ed] through the grounds,' exited near the southeast corner, and flowed into Garrison Creek near King Street. This creek — as a swale entering a masonry culvert — appears in 1868 and 1910 photographs of the eastern drive to the main entrance.[10]

The creeks on site were neither powerful nor picturesque, nor was the surrounding topography. J.C. Taché, reporting on his official inspection of the asylum in 1860, regretted its placement in 'the middle of a level tract in which no broken ground occurs to liven the prospect.'[11] A slight rise of land to the southwest apparently did little to break the general flatness and swampiness of the scene.[12] For more than a decade after it opened the massive building was the only focal point in a stark landscape whose ornamentation was just one of many priorities.

Boundary Demarcation

Fence-building was an early concern. A wooden fence and surrounding trench or 'Ha Ha' was constructed in 1846-47 to partially enclose the property.[13] Creation of a solid enclosure began in 1851 from Cumberland & Ridout's design for a front wall, east lodge, and east entrance gate.[14] Their wall, which rose at least ten feet above grade from a rubble stone foundation, was of white brick, with brick coping and brick-capped piers on either side. Directly in front of the main building, the masonry was lower but surmounted by an iron railing. Solid walls soon also stretched along the east and west boundaries; in his annual report for 1852 John Scott, the first medical superintendent, commented that the wall on three sides 'has added much to the privacy of the patients.'

By 1859, due to the porosity of the brick, the east and west walls were already undergoing extensive repairs. Accordingly, when Kivas Tully drew up plans in February 1860 for a masonry replacement for the wooden fence along the south boundary, he

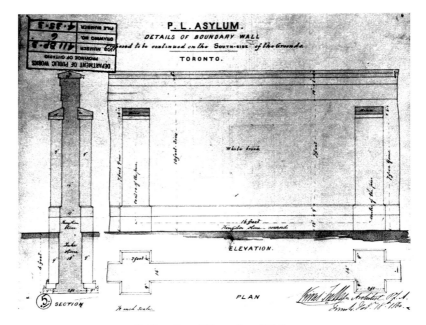

2. Details of Boundary Wall.
Archives of Ontario, RG 15-13-2-41, 411 BP-3, K-539

introduced stone copings for the wall and stone caps for the piers. With completion of this south wall in November 1861 the grounds were fully and, it was believed, permanently enclosed.

Yet the enclosures as originally built were anything but permanent. In 1888-89, following the government's sale to developers of twenty-four of the asylum's original fifty acres, the east and west boundary walls — about one thousand six hundred running feet — had to be removed from their original locations and reconstructed, from the old materials, 1) along the east side of Shaw Street and 2) east of the Dovercourt Road alignment. As had been the practice since the late 1840s, those male patients who were willing and able provided most of the labour.[16] Possibly as a result of this rebuilding, piers occur today only on the outsides of

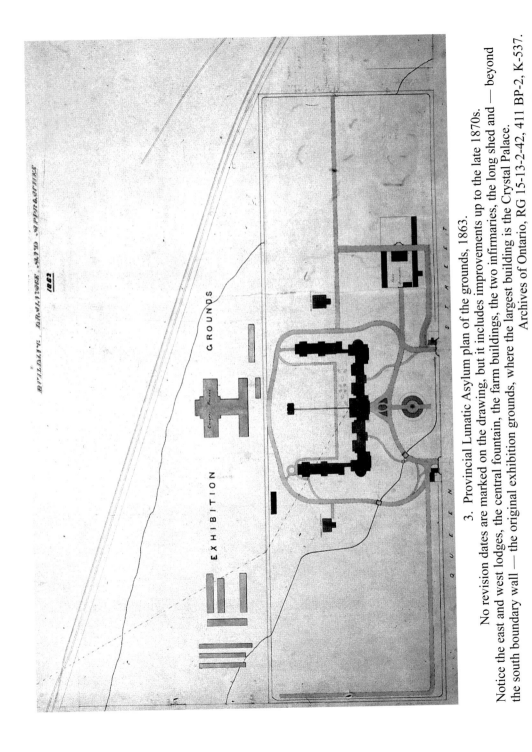

3. Provincial Lunatic Asylum plan of the grounds, 1863.
No revision dates are marked on the drawing, but it includes improvements up to the late 1870s.
Notice the east and west lodges, the central fountain, the two infirmaries, the long shed and — beyond
the farm buildings, the largest building is the Crystal Palace.
the south boundary wall — the original exhibition grounds, where the Archives of Ontario, RG 15-13-2-42, 411 BP-2, K-537.

the walls: an apparent deviation from the original design and certainly from Tully's scheme for the south wall.

Although less shattering than the loss of nearly half the property, many other events also affected these walls. In the 1890s, two long sheds were built against the south one, to the east and west of the powerhouse, finally replacing rotting and inflammable coal- and wood-storage sheds dangerously close to the main building.[17] These new fireproof structures, which incorporated brick from the original east and west walls, are now the only 19th-century buildings on the site.

Some changes to the walls came from a desire to open up views to and from the property. In 1878 a portion of the solid wall along Queen Street was made more transparent by the insertion, in front of the newly built medical superintendent's residence, of ornamental iron railing plus iron pedestrian and carriage gates.[18] A century later, the entire front wall was demolished and supplanted in part by the short, staggered stretch of modern cast-iron fencing that meets the east wall today.

The surviving walls exhibit other evidence of change. An 825-foot railway siding for coal deliveries that had to be accommodated during the 1929-40 period created the gap at the southwest corner now filled with wire-mesh fencing.[19] Three window-like openings in the south wall — between the present Grounds Building and the east shed — have been bricked in. The central section of this same wall has been demolished and replaced by wire-mesh fencing whose posts are set on the original foundation. Concrete copings have been substituted for stone ones atop portions of the east and west walls. A gateway near the north end of the west wall has been bricked in, leaving a visible reminder of the loss of fields to the west, the ensuing demise of the asylum farm itself, and the eventual removal of the stable yard and farm buildings originally served by this entrance.

Map of the Lunatic Asylum Toronto.

Asylum Ground 22 chains 75 links by 12 Chs 12 Lks containing 27 Acr. 2 Roods 12 Perches

Between Crawford, King and Shaw Street.

Between the South Wall of the Asyl. Ground and King Street.

In the Asylum Grounds

East: Orchard.

Between the Sup's Residence and Hospital in the Asylum Ground

West: Green Garden

two Plots together

Ornamental Ground 10

Arable Lands. Acres Roods Perch		
2.		16.
7.	1.	12
1		12
1		24.
1.		
2		
Total 13.	3.	24.

KING ST

Field

Field

Playground

Laundry Drying yd

Yard

Orchard

Field

Supt Residence

Field

Geo garden

Hospital

Field

SHAW ST

QUEEN ST.

Scale, 3⅞ chains 1 inch

CRAWFORD ST.

Field 2 Acres 16 Ps

4. Map of the Lunatic Asylum, Toronto, December 23, 1891.
There are now two long sheds against the south boundary wall.

Drives and Walkways

But to return to the 1840s: Besides fencing, another early concern was smoothing out natural and man-made irregularities. As early as July 1846 the Commissioners were awarding contracts 'for deep ploughing and levelling the Mounds on the grounds.'[20] John Howard (who in 1844 had laid out St. James Cemetery and the surroundings of Osgoode Hall and who had visited several newly landscaped asylums in the States) naturally envisioned a proper setting for this asylum. In January 1848 he wrote the Commissioners about 'the necessity of having the ground ploughed and levelled as early in the spring as possible.'[21] Not until March 1850, however, did he begin work on the 'plan for laying out PLA grounds' that he submitted in early April.[22]

Grading with hand-pushed tools and horse-drawn equipment was slow and laborious. At the end of 1850 John Scott reported 'the rough and uncultivated state of the grounds', and not until a year later could he state that 'a great amount of levelling has been completed.'[23] However smooth, the lawns were still subject to later disruption. During construction of Kivas Tully's east and west wings, for example, Joseph Workman, Scott's successor, wrote: 'Until the place is vacated by the builders, which I apprehend will not be before a couple of years more, it will be impossible to carry out the general plan [for the grounds] ...'[24]

Yet another concern was about proper approaches to the handsome new edifice. As early as 1848 Howard noted that the carriage drive could be 'Macadamized' by breaking 'chippings from the stone' of building construction.[25] It was 1851, however, before 'permanent roads' were laid down in front of the building, and 1854 before the patients had 'planked, or other walks' for the exercise already acknowledged as essential to their well-being.[26]

As the building complex grew within the walls so did the circulation system required to serve it: an evolution documented by successive site plans. There were other improvements. In 1877

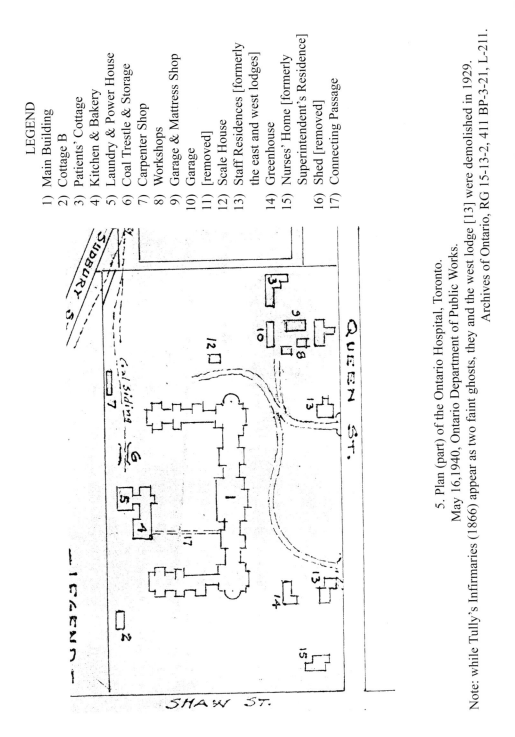

LEGEND

1) Main Building
2) Cottage B
3) Patients' Cottage
4) Kitchen & Bakery
5) Laundry & Power House
6) Coal Trestle & Storage
7) Carpenter Shop
8) Workshops
9) Garage & Mattress Shop
10) Garage
11) [removed]
12) Scale House
13) Staff Residences [formerly the east and west lodges]
14) Greenhouse
15) Nurses' Home [formerly Superintendent's Residence]
16) Shed [removed]
17) Connecting Passage

5. Plan (part) of the Ontario Hospital, Toronto.
May 16,1940, Ontario Department of Public Works.
Note: while Tully's Infirmaries (1866) appear as two faint ghosts, they and the west lodge [13] were demolished in 1929.
Archives of Ontario, RG 15-13-2, 411 BP-3-21, L-211.

third medical superintendent Daniel Clark was pleased to report the installation of 'a number of gas lamps...to light up the drive and sidewalks from the east gate to the main entrance.'[27] By 1897 he was asking for 'asphalt pavement' from the asylum to Queen Street and 'a great deal of sidewalk' to replace dangerously rotted boardwalks. Restating the need in 1904, he suggested laying down 'granolithic [concrete] pavements...instead of planks.' Not until about 1910, under fourth medical superintendent C.K. Clarke, was his predecessor's longstanding request realized.[28]

The Farm, Garden, and Orchard

In the spring of 1850 attention turned towards those parts of the enclosed grounds designated for food production. Much of the soil was so wet and heavy that draining it, in accordance with the best principles of scientific agriculture, was essential to good production. John Scott initiated the process and Joseph Workman carried it forward.[29] The first season's yield — 'a large store of carrots, parsnips, onions, beets, potatoes, beans, cabbages &c ... for the winter and spring' — was just a beginning. The crops mentioned in annual reports over the ensuing decades included animal fodder (clover, hay, oats, and timothy; field carrots and mangel wurtzel); a broad range of vegetables for immediate and later use (4850 bunches of asparagus and 490 bushels of tomatoes in 1889, for example); pot herbs (calendula or pot marigold, mint, parsley, sage, savory, and thyme); small fruits (citrons, currants, gooseberries, grapes, melons, raspberries, rhubarb, and strawberries); and apples (195 barrels in 1878). The livestock included draft horses, milk cows, laying hens, and hogs.[30]

In the oft-repeated opinions of the first three medical superintendents, the farm, garden, and orchard existed for several reasons. They produced most of the food for the asylum population. As a result, they made a significant contribution each year to the financial support of the institution. Equally important, they provided opportunities for selected patients to work with soil, plants, and animals, to breathe fresh air, and to get physical exercise: each of which was widely considered a valuable aspect of the care of the institutionalized and the treatment of some forms of mental illness. 'Improved and quiet' male patients with farming experience were prime candidates for outdoor work.[31] Women were given few such opportunities until 1918 when an acre of land around the convalescent hospital was fenced off to create a lawn and vegetable plot whose maintenance the women reportedly found 'quite a novelty...and one which they enjoyed.'[32] So late as 1949 the vegetable garden, lawns, and flower beds were offering patients 'useful occupation.'[33]

Due in part to the vagaries of weather and plant pests, the early medical superintendents' goals — of the asylum producing most of its own food while providing outdoor activity for suitable patients — remained perennially out of reach. The major limiting factor, however, was the inadequacy of the acreage for the number of residents. In his report for 1857 Joseph Workman observed what he, his successors, and provincial inspectors would repeat well into the next century: 'The quantity of land available for cul-

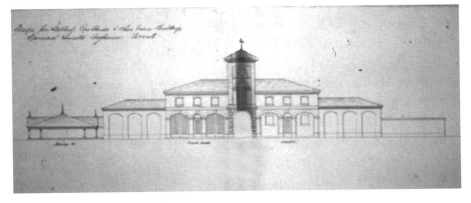

6. Design for Stabling, Cowhouse and other Farm Buldings.
Front (east) elevation, showing dairy, coach house and stable.
Archives of Ontario, C-11-59-0-1 (72) 3

tivation is inadequate to the wants and labour capability of the Asylum.'

In response, just one year later, 75 acres outside the enclosed grounds were leased to the asylum. Drained where necessary, they soon produced 'astonishing' crops.[34] A new land crisis arose, however, with completion of the wings, in 1868 and '70. Although the Toronto asylum ranked third in North America in terms of building size and patient population, it fell behind in terms of acreage. As Inspector J.W. Langmuir pointed out, an institution of its size should have 'at least 250 acres of land attached to it.'[35] In 1870, the Province, acting for the asylum, purchased from the Federal Government 150 acres in the Garrison Common to the south, between the Grand Trunk and Great Western railways. While Langmuir pursued the need for a bridge to carry patients safely over the tracks to the new holding, Joseph Workman organized crews to fight thistles, build board fences, and drain wetlands. Aided by the steward, he personally directed and mapped an extensive system of trenching and undertiling— especially in the northern part which had, just that spring, been 'so inviting to snipes and plover.'[36]

This gain of 150 acres was short-lived. Just one year later 30 of these acres were appropriated for the Central Prison and in 1878, an additional 600 square feet were taken for the Mercer Reformatory. Then, as the result of a land swap between the municipal and provincial governments in 1879, the asylum gained 19 acres on the former Crystal Palace grounds immediately beyond the south wall, but simultaneously lost a stretch of fields along the Dovercourt Road alignment.[37] A further assault on the asylum farm came in 1888 when, as previously mentioned, twenty-four of the original fifty acres were taken and the property reduced nearly to its present size. 'We have no farm, and only a few acres of garden ground,' Daniel Clark lamented in 1892.

For brief periods, the establishment of a branch asylum at

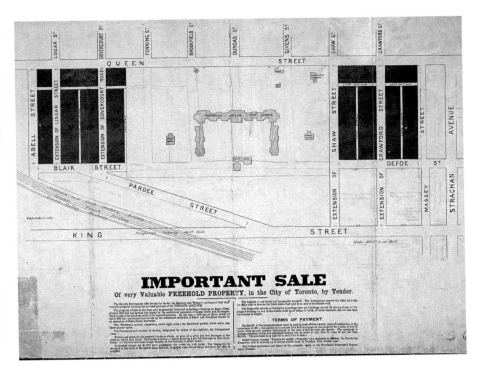

7. Important Sale Notice.
There is no date on this notice, but it is from the 1880s.
Archives of Ontario, RG 15-13-2-57, K 538

Mimico (later Lakeshore) in 1888 and of a new asylum at Whitby in 1912 seemed to answer the older institution's need for farm-land. So, too, would closing down the old asylum and moving to a larger site outside the city. Such a proposal was under serious consideration until the Great War — with its victims of shell shock and related disorders — put additional demands on all the existing facilities. As a consequence, the hospitals at Mimico and Whitby became independent (in 1892 and 1919 respectively) and kept most of their farm produce at home. The Toronto asylum had lost out once again. The one-acre vegetable garden inside the west wall, plus remnants of the one-acre twelve-perch apple orchard

8A. The Provincial Asylum, Toronto, C.W.
One of a stereoptical pair of views. The detached building on the left is
Tully's (east) free-standing infirmary, built in 1866. The Tully wings, com-
pleted in 1869, do not appear, although their foundations were begun in 1866.
Photographers: Armstrong, Beere & Hime, active in Toronto, 1855-61
City of Toronto Archives, SC 655-10

near the southeast corner, were then the only living reminders of
the institution's agricultural history.

The Ornamental Grounds

After fence building, ground levelling, road building, and
crop planting came ornamental landscaping. So early as October
1849, in fact, the Commissioners approved a request to 'employ'

some of the patients then housed at the Temporary Asylum by having them start 'improving and laying out the grounds' at the new site; but these earliest efforts focussed on rough grading.[39] Regarding further enhancement, the Directors of the new asylum cautioned in 1850 that 'a large sum' would be required for 'the perfecting of the grounds.'[40]

Perfection in landscape is an elusive goal. John Scott reported 'much progress' planting trees during his two and one-half year superintendency.[41] Joseph Workman carried the work forward throughout his 22 year tenure, overseeing the creation of mixed groves of evergreens and deciduous trees, as well as shrubberies and flower beds.

Many of the shade trees planted in the 19th century survived well into the 20th, when poor maintenance, disease, pollution, and natural attrition began taking their toll. Building projects have had a devastating effect. Former employee Emily Hopewell has written that in the mid-1950s '...the lovely old trees which were in the spacious grounds facing Queen Street were torn down to make

8B. (West) Free-Standing Infirmary. Two hospitals, each 60 feet in length by 235 feet in width, and three stories high, were built 200 feet east and west of the wings. They afforded accommodation for 30 patients each.

Their function was superseded when hospital wards were inserted between the main building and the wings in 1895. The free-standing former infirmaries were then used as cottages, and survived until 1929.

Reproduced by permission CAMH. AHCP&MHS

9. Panoramic Photograph, 1875.

This view shows the north face of the Asylum, from an observation point north of Queen Street, the observer standing on arable land. The ditch in the foreground may be indication of the waterlogged characteristics of the land. The scene encompasses all the ground from Ossington west almost to Dovercourt. The west lodge can be seen, a low building standing at the near side of the main entrance drive. The east lodge is also discernable, on the other side of the drive. The building at the extreme left is a pair of hous es on the east side of Fennings Street, built in 1874 by Lewis Richie.

The picture has been layered: the sky has been coloured a light yellow, trees have been added above the brick wall, particularly on the right in front of the farm buildings.

In 1875, acting on advice from Dr. Egerton Ryerson, the Provincial Legislature author ized an entry for the province in the International Exposition of 1876, to be held in

delphia, Pennsylvania. School trustees were asked to send specimens of student
to the project co-ordinator, Dr. May. Photographs were taken of the exterior and
or of various school buildings, to show their 'style and character.'
o included in the exhibit were views of other public buildings, such as jails and asy-
. An earlier numbering scheme indicates that there were originally at least 130 photo-
s in the collection. Of that number, 59 survive at the Archives of Ontario.
oramic photograph above by Hunter, [Rose] & Co., who carried out a substantial
nt of photographic and printing work for the Government of Ontario. An engraving
ater made from this photograph and published in the *Weekly Globe* of 30 August
, and in J. Ross Robertson's *Landmarks of Toronto*.
rchives of Ontario, #74 Special Report, Sessional Papers 44, 1877, B97, Reel 10; and
Archives of Ontario, L 107

way for the new [reception] building.'[42] Still, in 1961, east and west of the Howard building and Tully wings, there remained three elms and one horse chestnut with whopping four-foot girths, and fourteen elms, horse chestnuts, and maples nearly as big, at three to three and one-half feet in diameter.[43] Many of those trees later succumbed to old age and Dutch elm disease; and the demolition and construction of the 1970s meant additional losses. Replacements around the new buildings include scattered white birches, dense stands of Austrian pines, and rows of ginkgos typical of that period.

The quadrangle, in the area created by the addition of east and west wings and easily seen from windows on three sides, was in the 19th century a valued part of the ornamental grounds, as were the side lawns. The park-like space between the front wall and the main building, however, received the most attention. Plantings that appeared sparse in photographs from the 1860s had become lush by the late 1870s. A guide to the city published in 1878 described the asylum as 'inclosed in the midst of very fine grounds and flower gardens.'[44]

The ornamental portions of the grounds have at various times accommodated sleigh rides, picnics, strawberry festivals, garden parties, annual sports days, croquet, lawn and court tennis, bowling on the green, baseball and softball, and calisthenics. In the early decades, patients likely to attempt escape were taken out in walking parties (from which they occasionally escaped anyway, usually by climbing one of the walls). Sometime before 1900, enclosure of an 'airing ground' allowed these individuals less-supervised access to the outdoors. Many patients have apparently always been free to walk unaccompanied.[45]

From 1860 into the early 1900s, three cast-iron fountains embellished the grounds.[46] For the larger one it is likely that Kivas Tully adapted the illustration in a manufacturer's catalogue when drafting the peacocks and dolphins on its pedestal. Placed at

P.L. ASYLUM.

DESIGN FOR FOUNTAIN TO BE ERECTED.

ON THE NORTH FRONT OF THE BUILDING

ELEVATION.

10. Design for a Fountain.
This fountain was designed for the prominent position in front of the main drive into the Asylum.
Archives of Ontario, RG 15-113-2-41, 411 BP-3, K-539

the intersection of the drives to the main entrance, its three tiers were clearly visible from Queen Street. The two smaller fountains, standing 176 feet apart some 65 feet from the rear of the main building, provided focal points in the long, mirror-image parterres within the quadrangle. In 1893, when construction of the chapel/amusement/work hall disrupted this area, they were moved close to the main entrance. Later artifacts to grace the front lawn have ranged from an ornamental birdbath, circa 1950, to *Cutouts*, the competition-winning wood sculpture by Colette Whiten that stood near the northeast corner from 1978 until late 1993.[47]

Lawns and trees have been constant elements of the ornamental landscape. More ephemeral, floral displays have included dense, well-rounded shrubberies in front and hedges and parterres in the quadrangle, in the 1860s and '70s; crescent-shaped beds filled with annuals of one colour edged with another, around

11. North Face, circa 1877.
Gas lamps were installed on the asylum grounds and on Queen Street in 1877, which helps establish the date of this photograph. The fountain can be seen in place, at the far right.
Reproduced by permission CAMH, AHCP&MHS

1900; tiered circles with cannas at their centre, in the 1930s; perennial borders ablaze with lilies and roses, circa 1940; a so-called 'Japanese garden' composed of horizontal junipers, chipped brick, and precast pavers, in the late 1970s; weed-free mass plantings in the courtyards at the start of the '90s; and 'I[heart]CAMH' spelled out with clipped evergreens in 1999-2000.[48]

A refreshing innovation of the 1990s has been the involvement of people from the community at large. The Heritage Garden Project, envisioned by staff member Steven Hughes in 1992 and partially funded by grants from the Evergreen and Friends of the Environment foundations, brought together staff, students, clients, and neighbours. Mass-planted junipers soon shared space with native trees, shrubs, grasses, and wildflowers chosen to attract butterflies and hummingbirds. During the same period, nearby residents also created a community garden east of the greenhouse, a wildflower garden beside the tennis court, and — in the summer of 1999 — a zucchini-covered arbour on the front lawn.[49] What next?

Conclusion

History teaches that this landscape, like any other, is subject to change. It is important to identify those elements, both above and below ground, that merit preservation and/or documentation. The city of Toronto has designated the walls, but the two sheds remain vulnerable and all the old masonry needs conservation.[50] No current tree inventory or ongoing program of tree maintenance and renewal exists, although community gardener Martin Rudd has proposed creating one.[51] Over half the original 50 acres have been lost, but those that remain include valuable pieces of Toronto's built and open-space heritage: a legacy from those who began working these grounds more than 150 years ago.

12. The Asylum Conservatory.
Showing (above) east elevation, with two story verandah addition, (below) a display of growing plants. Located behind the East Lodge, this greenhouse provided activity and a source of continuing interest for patients for many years.
Glass negatives, reproduced by permission CAMH, AHCP&MHS

. FOUR .

BUILDING

CANADA WEST

by Alec Keefer

ON JUNE 25 1849 the opera, *La Sonnambula* was performed at St. Andrew's Masonic Hall on the second floor above a hotel at the corner of Church and Colborne Streets. That opera, along with *Norma*, were favourites with the local concert-going public. The composer of both, Vincenzo Bellini (1802 – 1835) held that 'pure melody, the simple nobility and beauty of song'[1] was one of his goals. He strove to free music of the artificially contrived and dense complexity of structure that typified western music after the Baroque era.

Seated in the hall that night with a party of friends was John George Howard. Howard, the most successful Toronto architect of his generation, who would live until 1890, was a mere six years from retiring to his farm in the country near the Humber River. That night he was preoccupied with completing a long list of projects. These included his largest, and his best building: The Provincial Asylum.

The performance over, Howard would drive his chaise cart home past all the farms along Queen Street West, out to his unassuming but beloved cottage, 'the Lodge.' Still ringing in his ears would have been the last tune sung that night: the Rondo from the Aria, '*Ah ! non giunge uman pensiero.*' The chorus of villagers beseech the catatonic heroine, Amina, to wake and return to the land of the living from her vale of fears and tears.

1. John George Howard (1803-90).
Watercolour on paper,
Artist: Thomas H. Stevenson,
circa 1847-48.
From the collection of the City of Toronto, Culture Division,
John George Howard Collection [1978.41.504]

Hail Amina, wake to gladness
Hail Amina, wake to joy
From this day your sorrow's o'er, yes
From this day your sorrow's o'er.

Oh, recall not one earthly sorrow,
With the bliss of heav'n around us
An illusion it was that bound us ...

Hand in hand while on earth we wander
We will form a heav'n of love[2]

As Howard passed his Asylum that night it would have been still cloaked in darkness under a canopy of the stars, with only the night watchman in possession. This mountain of brick and stone awaited its completion. The government of the Canadas that had ordered its construction and the commissioners charged with realizing that task, would not be disappointed. No, this building was a unique by-product. For broad societal changes contributed much to the character and quality of the design and the plan. Aspects of Howard's career had made him keenly aware of these changes and capable of achieving the desired program. Bellini's chorus is a very fitting anthem to keep in mind as we begin considering the plan, the design and building of The Provincial Lunatic Asylum.

It was the purpose of the musical style adopted by Bellini to elevate pathos *by curtailing the redundant ornament.*[3] Further, for the story-lines of his plots, the composer did not look to myths or fairy tales nor to the domestic irregularities of the minor nobility, then the norm in the arts. No, Bellini looked to life itself; he set *La Sonnambula* in a village in Switzerland. And there, the lowly villagers are the ones who know the truth. Bellini, like Howard, was a 'modernist'; like many proponents of 'the new' he was free to create art , without obeying the heavy canon of tradition and of mere practice. This, then is the cultural background against which we must see the Asylum on Queen St West rise. But what of the bigger picture ?

Civil society in Canada West, about 1830

When Howard stepped off the lake schooner onto the pier on 11 September 1832 at York (Toronto), some residents could still remember when the town site was densely forested. In 1830 with a population of only 5,000, over 300 buildings were under construction. While some were redbrick, many were merely frame — only a handful were of stone. Rudimentary buildings, two rooms up and two rooms down, that simply provided shelter. Usually with steep gable-ended roofs, few had graceful lines or ornamentation. All these structures had been by-and-large drawn up by the builders, men such as John Ewart. A few had been sketched by gentlemen, but architects had no influence on the community.

This 1830 town was contained south of the Street we call Queen between Parliament and Yonge. Over the next decade, as the community spread west, away from the Don River past York Street toward Spadina, each year would see the start of at least 400 structures — still most were frame but increasingly they were redbrick and symmetrical, echoing faintly the classicism so prevalent in Howard's Britain.

Yet only a few years after he arrived, by 1835 this community, with City status in hand and now renamed Toronto, had doubled its population to 10,000. This rapid pace of growth meant that the wilderness was constantly being pushed back. Acre after acre needed to be cleared and subdivided; the land levelled and drained; road allotments established and sewer lines installed. Howard, the surveyor, was open for business.

The citizenry of this new town did not intend it to remain a backwater. They demonstrated this by such acts of public spiritedness as the incorporation of the Mechanics Institute in 1831.

2. Design for a Government House in Toronto, cost £50,000.
Watercolour and ink on paper, perspective drawing,
Artist: John George Howard, circa 1833.
From the collection of the City of Toronto, Culture Division, John George Howard Collection [1978.41.92]

This precursor of the free public library was an essential compo- nent of a well-run community that held itself to be the possessor of a brilliant future. Howard felt at home.

Granted, there was still no free education. As yet in many churches the pews were rented by the year. And health care was spartan; the hospital was never intended for the entire population. Only the deserving poor would be admitted — and they were expected to contribute toward their maintenance. The ill who were well established were cared for at home by their families.

To a large degree the built-form of the City of Toronto in 1840 reminded Howard of any number of smaller British provin- cial towns. The social and cultural institutions would also be mod- eled on what had evolved over there. The sole difference would be in the huge waves of immigrants and the massive new building that those numbers necessitated. But that was precisely one of the many factors that had motivated Howard to immigrate.

The political re-organization of Upper Canada and Lower Canada by the British Government that was the reaction to the unrest of the late 1830s ensured that public building projects would be forthcoming and advanced — governmental and insti- tutional, affording any well- placed, politically sensitive architect greater opportunities in scope not readily available in Britain to one of Howard's back-ground. Howard arrived fully capable of playing a leading role in the building of Canada West.

British Architecture during the Regency

We find mankind restless and dissatisfied [sic], and strain- ing every faculty of mind and body for the improvement of their condition   (1821)[4]

The London, England that Howard left on 25 June 1832 had, during his own early days, taken on some of the look that we know as that City's built form today: row after row of attached

3. Design for the University of Queen's College.
Watercolour on paper, panoramic view, high pavilion over central roof, central porch with roof pediment, signed and dated 'J.G. Howard, 1835'.
From the collection of the City of Toronto, Culture Division, John George Howard Collection [1978.41.90]

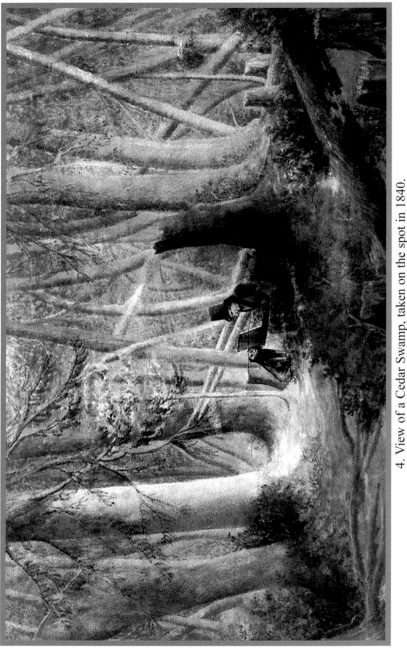

4. View of a Cedar Swamp, taken on the spot in 1840.
Watercolour on paper, artist John George Howard.
From the collection of the City of Toronto, Culture Division, John George Howard Collection [1978.41.100]

terraces of houses, often fronting onto squares. Earlier versions were built using London's own local brick, the best were the buff coloured; later ones would be covered in stucco. All this building activity was so unprecedented then, that it was termed quite simply, the 'improvements.'[5] The government of the day had, at the instigation of the Prince Regent, for the first time played a role in this scheme of urban renewal.

Other arts responded to this climate. They began to show, over time, a growth in informality — greater warmth and more human. In portraiture we see a heightened sensitivity to the character of the individual and the specific situation and much less reliance on the poses associated with classicism.

These initiatives were an early by-product of the century of peace — the 'Pax Britannica' in Europe that followed the defeat of Napoleon. In this period of stability, trade and commerce thrived. At last money was available. But also people were more open and relaxed. They felt freer to engage in discussions about all manner of issues and theories. Controversies raged between different religious doctrines such as that between the Established Church (Anglicans) and the Dissenters (Methodists).

The staid Rationalism of the previous century tried to withstand the flowering of the new Romanticism. Both these camps held that Nature was now non-threatening. Rationalism *reasoned* it so, while romanticism *felt* it be so. This struggle was not just over ideas but also over value systems. Personal 'happiness' was thought to be universally possible and was indeed the normal state for human existence. Bromides offered that love could bring one safely 'through sleep and darkness.'[6]

Intellectual heavyweights of the day weighed in. In 1837, Coleridge held that:

The permanency of the nation...and personal freedom... depend on a continuing and progressive civilization. But civilization [he warns] is itself a mixed good...the hectic of disease...the bloom of health...[true civilization, he offers, is] in the harmonious development of those qualities and faculties that characterize our humanity.[7]

According to Raymond Williams, the poet takes Civilization to mean the general condition of 'a state or habit of mind.' Williams maintains that the use of that word in this way represented a redefined meaning

In this economic and cultural climate the profession of Architect came to resemble more closely what we understand it to be today. This was true in London where firms were vying for building projects, each headed by a principal with social and political connections. A strong collegial environment emerged and this encouraged, indeed ensured, that there would be both public and private critical awareness of economics, efficiency and of the structures themselves.

As to the designs, the cold formal approach of that we term Palladian at first gave way rather naturally to its more flexible descendant Neo-classicism. One architect is more associated with this new wave than any other, John Nash. Howard would have been very familar with the long list of Nash's projects. Many were remarkable for not only did he have the breadth of vision so that his terrace 'improvements' show remarkable flexibility and versatility but he also was one of the first 'moderns' to arrive at broad fundamentals of town-planning. His Regent Park scheme in London was termed 'a glory to the government, which will be more felt by remote posterity than the victories of Trafalgar and Waterloo.'[8]

The triumphs of Nash's terraces are many. It was not just that his terraces are so pleasing in their simplicity and variety but also their plans are logical. Another triumph was the building-process itself which proved logistically, very successful in the manufacture, supply and delivery of materials. Strict control of the construction process and site was important. Maintaining a high level of consistency during construction of a terrace 600 foot long was no mean feat.

Finally Nash was not merely designing a series of large buildings that were or were not individually, great architecture. Rather he understood his task was to build a new, great imperial city. Thus the total vision he realized — an imposing backdrop against which one could hope to live a convenient, meaningful and valuable life — was greater than the sum of the individual buildings.

Architects of Howard's generation sought practical solutions to newly identified complex problems — sanitation, ventilation, heating. They would work *with* suppliers to select material to be referenced in the detailed specifications. Site visits to the brick-field, lime kiln and quarry were regular parts of the work week. They would need to know enough about the skills and crafts of the various trades to guarantee quality of workmanship. A sharp eye and a good memory for details were needed on their regular visits to the construction site. And, they had to develop superior communications skills as they led the team that would realize these great undertakings.

In general, the overall design for housing would be a 'dressed-down' or plain classicism. Improvisation could be encouraged though, and the detail could be lively and vigourous. This innovative approach extended beyond residential projects, and the built-form in other sectors — the corporate and the institutional — could not always be readily distinguished on the exterior from the domestic. One of the exceptions to this rule would be when the agencies or organizations had deep historic association. Then something 'old English' in appearance, like say 'Tudor' could be used.

This society was also keenly interested in improvements to the social order. At first entirely charitable in nature, all manner of facilities were established and buildings constructed to house those in need. There were orphanages, almshouses, hospitals and so on. Often these establishments were the result of efforts by philanthropic individuals who wanted to explore alternative treatments. In the best cases, patterns and approaches to care were considered in a systematic manner. Great strides were made to treat individuals more humanely. As a result much thought started to go into the interior design and layout of these institutions.

By the time St Luke's Hospital appeared in the London of 1750 it was understood by many that institutions worked best when patients were subjected to interrelated principles and processes such as grouping by classification and segregation. The best regimes were concerned about hygiene, diet, regular exercise and therapy. With the passing by the Parliament of the Municipal Reform Legislation in 1831, English society could begin to look to local governments rather than to the Church to form and regulate dedicated care systems and programs. This is the context in which Howard was trained to be an architect and compassionate modernist.

Howard's Lunatic Asylum

Although the moderns have not made many additions to the art of building, with respect to mere beauty of ornament, yet it must be confessed they have carried simplicity, convenience, and neatness of workmanship, to a very great degree of perfection, particularly in England; where plain good sense hath preferr'd these more necessary parts of beauty, which everyone can understand, to that richness of taste which is so much to be seen in other countries, and so often substituted in their room.

William Hogarth, *The Analysis of Beauty,* (1753)[9]

5. Building the Asylum.

November 11, 1848
Morning writing out order for Mr. Garth. Mr Daly called and said that the
Commissioners were going to look over the Asylum at half past ten. To
Chewett at quarter to eleven with him in our chaise to the Asylum. Met the
Commissioners there. Mr Baldwin was also there and said that he thought it
likely that the wings would be commenced when the other part was finished.
At half past three with Mr. Chewett to Lot 35. Home at half past five.
J.G. Howard, Journal entry

Seen in the picture are, from left: Premier Baldwin; three Commissioners
including J.G.Chewett; and, architect J.G.Howard.

Watercolour on paper
Artist: August Köllner, 1848
Signed and dated
Reproduced by permission National Gallery and CAMH, AHCP&MHS

It is hard for us today to realize the magnitude of the commitment that the government was making when it set out to build an asylum of the size proposed. One of the best ways to come to terms with that is to compare it with the other public buildings of its generation. The people of the city in fact would wait 40 years to see a building of the scale and magnificence of Howard's. And that would be Toronto's third City Hall, by E. J. Lennox.

At 584 ft — 8 chains and 56 feet — the asylum was the largest public non-military building in the nation. Howard's task was to ensure that it did not appear a monolith. While at first glance it must not be a threatening place yet it should be taken seriously. For as a residential clinic where the ill were to be cured, neither should it be frivolous — a mere resort. Basing his design on the terrace pattern he would know well from London, his creation would remind some of an assemblage of 'many mansions.'

The structure, based on the open quadrangle design of Cambridge university, had two principal profiles — the public profile seen from the north, down Dundas [Ossington] Street and also along Queen Street coming from the east or the west. The more private face from the south would seldom be seen by the public but would be the one known best by the patients.

The setback from the property line on Queen Street and the placement of the building in the centre of the site was established to remove the building from the hustle and bustle of the day-to-day. The building was four storeys tall with an attic. The exterior walls, made of specially selected cream-white brick, looked sound and solid. They were plain and smooth. From the street , the building in many ways would seem to be quiet.

And, while not severe, Howard's design is certainly understated. The architect achieves this by visually breaking the facade up into a series of sections. In a predictable pattern, every other section is recessed slightly behind the wall of the central block. The alternate sections are ranked: the end ones, on the extreme east and west, are slightly more prominent than those mid-building. The pattern of these strong vertical right-angled corners produces shadow lines. This is balanced by secondary horizontal components: the first and second floors contained within a unifying brick frame. The third and fourth floors are treated individually in the same manner. Yet the materials used are absolutely consistent on all the parts. And so the massing of the huge structure is fluid or organic — truly the sum of its parts.

On all sections the windows are identical in shape by floor level. This pattern holds on the central block although some windows here were larger. There is a single entrance that is in the central block, administration section. This is in line with, but not directly under the dome which itself is comfortably recessed back, so that it rides over the spinal column of the asylum — the exceedingly wide great central hall. This is dictated in part by sound engineering and in part to seem less threatening.

It is interesting to note that when Howard was required to scale back the building after construction was underway, his reaction was typical. He chose to simplify the program curtailing what little ornamentation he had prescribed: Limestone quoins disappear from corners and pilasters are now of brick. There were other changes that he would not have welcomed.

Howard's building as constructed never reflected what Howard intended when he won the contest in 1844. This should not surprise us as this is normal under such design process conditions. Howard's grand scheme was but **half** completed. Notwithstanding repeated promises to the contrary, the east, and west wings, when they were put up, were done to some else's plan (see the paper by Steven Bell).

Howard's plan was for a building that would be well-defined, logical and clear to all who approached and especially to those who entered. The prevailing impression, inside and out, should be calm and not distracting. Visitors to the site, if curious and perceptive, would realize that the various sections articulated on the exterior in brick and stone related directly to different uses in the rooms behind the facade.

To Paris and Back

On 30April 1853 Howard and this wife Jemima left Toronto for Europe via New York City. They were on a three month tour of Europe that coincided with his 50th birthday. The true motivating factor had been a protracted, expensive and upsetting legal battle with Samuel Jarvis over the considerable fees that Howard maintained he was owed for 5 years work, surveying Jarvis property. Howard's own physician and Jemima were convinced that unless he got away, the strain would break him utterly.

Soon after Howard arrived in Toronto, back in 1832 he had done a watercolour after an illustration showing the fall of the Bastille and the freeing of the prisoners. It occupied a place of honour on the walls of his studio. Not many of Howards clients would have tolerated it in their parlors.

The Paris of 1853 that Howard visited was alive with excitement. Not only had France survived the tumultuous years of revolution — 1847 to 1849, but new building — public buildings were going up. How excited Howard must have been to be there at that moment to inspect closely these modern monuments, as the Paris we know today was rising all around him. The best designers were on the threshold of true change. 'Around the year 1830 there emerged in Paris a group ... with a new, precise method of spatial and structural analysis. This permitted them to grasp the subject in terms of its organic principles.' 'In the end it produced a space that is utterly and unmistakable [utilitarian].'[10]

Most of the the examples Howard would see in 1853 can be termed 'abstract classicism': Duban's École des Beaux Arts (1832-40); and Labrouste's Bibliothèque Sainte Geneviève (1844-50). About the latter it has been said that he 'understood that architectural meaning had not just to be communicated, but to be embodied.'[11] Both of these designers were in the vanguard of the movement that was to evolve in the Second Empire architectural style.

While Howard was in Paris he may have met Labrouste. In the following spring, on February 16 to be exact, Labrouste would be appointed architect for the Salle des Imprimés (1869 - 70) which is reckoned his masterpiece. For 'Labrouste embodiment in the [library of the] Salle des Imprimés is transparent. It is not a setting for thought, it is thought itself.'[12]

Likewise the Provincial Asylum as designed by John George Howard as he himself said was *not* a place of 'incarceration;' it was instead the embodiment of a powerful and humane value system. This concept may not have been completely understood by its proponents in Canada West as the rafters rose on the south side of Queen Street. Nevertheless, the struggle to effect changes necessary to reach Coleridge's 'civilization' continues. Howard did achieve one of the best physical environments in which to advance the cure of those with mental illness. His approach to the design was in part driven by his humanity. He was determined to

6. A Greek Temple. Drawn by Howard in 1885, possibly while on a return visit to England.

From the collection of the City of Toronto, Culture Division, John George Howard Collection [1978.41.502]

do as he was charged: deliver well-lit, ventilated, private and comfortable spaces to promote the restoration of rational behaviour and the return of those after treatment to society.[13] His achievements became blurred when under successive regimes his building was host to different agendas. This does not lessen our respect for his truly 'modern' achievement. For Howard's Asylum 'it is the representation, the setting, the cloak of its function.'

A Note on Perspective Drawing by Edna Hudson

A freehand sketch, sometimes in perspective, is much used by architects to give first embodiment to their ideas. Before the end of the 18th century, such a sketch would also suffice to communicate design ideas to clients. Architectural drawings — the plans and elevations — were produced both to instruct tradesmen through the construction phase, and to describe to the client the building program. But the impression of the building that an untutored layman can derive from architectural drawings is often vague.

The true perspective drawing is derived from plans and elevations before the building is realized. It is an accurate representation of what the eye will see after construction is complete. The perspective drawing is a useful bridge between the architect and client, it often 'makes the sale', as was understood more and more clearly after the invention of photography.[14]

Drawings of the Provincial Asylum would have been made for government appointed commissioners and members of the military to examine (see paper by Shirley Morriss). Much discussion would have centred on points of organization of the building, the building program, rather less on the aesthetics of the building design. In proof of which, one notices that there are at least three different floor plans for the Asylum extant, which all have the same footprint, but what the rooms are to be used for varies, and some of the room appointments.

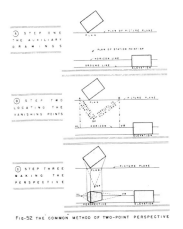

7. Diagram. Shows derivation of perspective drawing from plan and elevations.

FIG-52 THE COMMON METHOD OF TWO-POINT PERSPECTIVE

The skill level and influence of British military topographers was strong in the early 19th century, following the appointment of watercolourist Paul Sandby as an instructor at the army training school at Woolwich in 1786. Officers in the Royal Engineers were trained to prepare maps and elevations, and many developed into very competent watercolourists while on their tour of duty in Canada.[15] The various watercolour societies that Howard helped to organize had a number of military men among their members. With respect to architecture, Howard was well prepared to respond to everything that the questioning mind of a military topologist might ask.

Perspective drawings are part of the process of rational design, today made freely available by the widespread use of computer-aided design. Our facility with technique has exposed the perspective drawing as the deceptive device it can be — often because an unavailable observation point has been selected, or surrounding buildings left out. There are also more subtle methods available to mislead, such as slanted or curved picture planes, but the labour of calculation involved is prohibitive. Howard used perspective drawings quite often. Whenever he needed to assure himself of the correctness of his intention with respect to a design, he would draw a small perspective to satisfy himself on the argument. Examples in Howard's papers show the placement of a house chosen for its view from a vantage point, and the design of roof levels and shapes studied for picturesque effect.

Howard did two perspective drawings of the Asylum that have survived. One from the rear, the South View, and one from an angle in front, the North View. They are each drawn on paper about 14 3/4" x 10" which is not large for the amount of work required. (The elevations and plans that Howard drew as working drawings were on larger sheets of paper, at least 25" x 32" and the scale was about 20 feet to the inch, as opposed to 150 feet to the inch for the perspectives) The rendered perspective in each case occurs near the centre of the paper.

Let us examine the North View in more detail. Low on the page is the plan of the Asylum, turned at 20 degrees to the picture plane, which is a horizontal line intersecting the north-west corner of the building. This arrangement will give a laterally inverted image, acceptable only because the building is symmetrical. Usually the plan is drawn at the top of the page, but the perspective will do better as a presentation drawing if the top of the page is empty. The plan is finely drawn in ink with a very sure hand. Although the lines do not meet exactly at every corner, one needs a magnifying glass to detect it.The line of sight is located perpendicular to the picture plane, intersecting at the northwest corner of the building. The finished perspective appears on the centre of the page, derived from the plan as follows: some faint, fine pencil lines are drawn from various projections of the building to the station point, otherwise known as the eye of an observer. Where these lines cut the picture plane, vertical planes of the building are defined in accurate perspective to the observer at station point. Clearly the observer is standing on Queen Street, approaching the Asylum. It is difficult now to be sure exactly how many feet the Asylum was set back from Queen Street, but something over 300 feet is true by all accounts, including the evidence of this drawing.

The horizon line is drawn parallel to the picture plane indeed, and drawn across the centre of the page, very close to where Howard is going to draw the building, only 3/16" from it. This is correct because the ground is level. Architects nowadays usually choose a high horizon line, the building as a bird would see it. This is done so that you can see more of the roof, but Howard keeps the observer's feet on the ground, which is less to worry about because he does not want to show us much of the roof. What part of it we can see is entirely devoid of chimney pots, so the design has not got to that detail yet, though there are two pretty cupolas. The perpendiculars (from the picture plane to the horizon line) are next to be drawn. From the observer, lines are now drawn parallel to each side of the building plan, until these lines intersect the picture plane. From there a line perpendicular to the picture plane rises to the horizon line and defines the right and left vanishing points. The heights of the building should properly be projected from elevations placed to either side of the line of sight. There are no elevations drawn on this paper, so Howard simply used the scale of the plan and height he knew to give measurements along the line of sight which is the eastern corner of the finished drawing of the building.

Tiny details, just a stroke to represent a window for example, complete the representation of the building. Add a few tiny lines to represent boats sailing on the lake on either side, brush in a couple of hayricks or sheds, then a few large bushes to disguise any awkwardness in the front and we are done. It is convincing, and so why argue?

Perspective drawings were not commonly done by architects at the time.[16] The conventions of perspective had been discovered early in the Renaissance, and used by artists since, but not architects. It is said by Berger[17], that 'perspective makes the single eye

Provincial Lunatic Asylum.

North View. J. G. Howard. *Architect. Toronto.*

8. Provincial Lunatic Asylum, North View.

the centre of the visible world' thus the picture drawn in perspective shows 'the visible world is arranged for the spectator as the universe was once thought to be arranged for God' which gives a feeling of great personal power to the viewer, even though there may also be a feeling of dread attached. In simpler terms, it can be said that a perspective drawing appeals to egotistic feelings that are universal, and thus influences people of any background.

This drawing, on a miniature scale, gives the viewer a glimpse of the finished building. It is so delicately done, it encourages romantic reflection — we feel the level ground; the presence of nature in the strongly marked vegetation and the glow of the setting sun on the north face of the building fills us with the contentment of a beautiful midsummer evening. A careful use of shades of grey, some ochre, and fine detail confirm this aura of romantic preciousness.

Yet what was the purpose of this drawing? The finish is so highly worked that it must have been prepared for an audience, perhaps the commissioners, to produce in their minds 'the impression of the building as a whole as he [the architect] conceived it.'[18] This example appeals to introspective thought; it does not have the general viewer impact it could have because it is so small. It also fails to exploit the obvious visual attraction of the building's outline, which is that the building appeared to fold and unfold as one approached. True, the Asylum was located so far from Queen Street that the unfolding of the building could be seen most powerfully when a person approaching by road was still half a mile away, possibly at the original 50 acre boundary. If one was on the asylum grounds, approaching the building not from Queen Street but along a nearer path in front of the asylum, then the unfoldings could be seen when one was less distant. We have no doubt that Howard fully understood this property of the building profile he had chosen. But these effects would need several perspective drawings to convey, and Howard did not attempt it. The movie camera, which has again transformed our expectations of what drawings can do, was yet some years away.

For the first Parliament buildings competition in Ottawa in 1859,[19] several contestants entered perspective drawings among their other competition drawings, though only 'elevations, plans, sections, specifications, and estimates' were required. As the designs were large and complex, involving many vanishing points, it is likely that special draughtsmen were employed to work out the details.[20] The contributing plans and elevations do not show. Some competition perspectives were highly coloured, and all included staffage. All were intended to attract attention.

The determination to unite Canada gave tremendous power to the engineers who built the roads, railroads and bridges that were required. The judges for the Parliament buildings competition were two engineers, Samuel Keefer and Frederick Rubidge. Such judges made clear their desire to see a realistic representation of the building that was to be, as well as program and construction details.

Howard's perspective drawings for clients set a precedent. When he used his skills in measured drawing and geometry to show his proposed new building and its positioning to clients, Howard had set his face towards the future, and led the profession.

. FIVE .

JOHN GEORGE HOWARD
ARCHITECT

by Shirley Morriss

As FAR AS IS KNOWN JOHN GEORGE HOWARD was the first trained architect to practice in the Town of York (Toronto). During his professional life he made a notable contribution to the city's built environment and fulfilled commissions elsewhere in the province and in Quebec. As a surveyor and engineer he participated in Toronto's development, as an artist he enhanced cultural life, and he is fondly remembered for the gift of his home and property to Toronto's citizens.[1]

He was born John Corby in 1803 in Hertfordshire, England. In his account of his career, *Incidents in the Life of John G. Howard, Esq.* (Toronto, 1885), he tells how at the age of about seventeen he began working as a carpenter and joiner, also acquiring a knowledge of surveying, engineering, and architecture. In 1824 he was taken on as an articled clerk by London architect William Ford, and was eventually permitted to engage in business for himself. Then owing to the 'distress of the times and the sparsity of building operations' he sought greater opportunity through emigration to Upper Canada.

In 1827 he married Jemima Frances Meikle, the daughter of a surveyor. Shortly before they left England he changed his name to John George Howard. After a perilous journey across the Atlantic in 1832 the Howards settled in York to endure an impoverished first winter in rented quarters. During these months he prepared a set of architectural drawings that in 1833 led Lieutenant Governor Sir John Colborne to arrange for his appointment as drawing master at Upper Canada College where he taught until 1856.[2] The position assured a regular income and useful contacts with students' families — potential clients. Regarded with 'affectionate respect' by his students, he occasionally involved them in other aspects of his work: in 1847–48 they assisted him with surveys for a topographical plan of Toronto. He also provided architectural services to the college and he designed the cast-iron lamps that still ornament the grounds.

Newcomers with professional status were in demand in the thriving community. Howard was soon busy with surveys and the building of wharves, bridges, and in the 1840s with industrial buildings such as William Gamble's Humber River mill, and the Ontario Brewery on Front Street. From 1843 to 1855 he was employed as city surveyor to lay out streets and sidewalks, superintend planking and paving and the installation of sewers[3]. In 1846 he charted the Toronto harbour [4]

Early on his architectural practice included commercial structures reminiscent in style of the late Georgian mode that he would have known in England. The red brick Chewett Buildings built in 1834 at the corner of King and York Streets combined shops, offices, apartments, and an inn and tavern. It was the town's first office block.[5] The same year he designed the Canada Company offices and built a 'cottage villa' for Thomas Mercer Jones, a company official. He designed hotels, warehouses and commercial rows of from two to four storeys divided into stores with yards at the rear. He gave Victoria Row, completed in 1842 on King Street East, architectural presence by raising the centre unit to a pedimented fourth storey.[6]

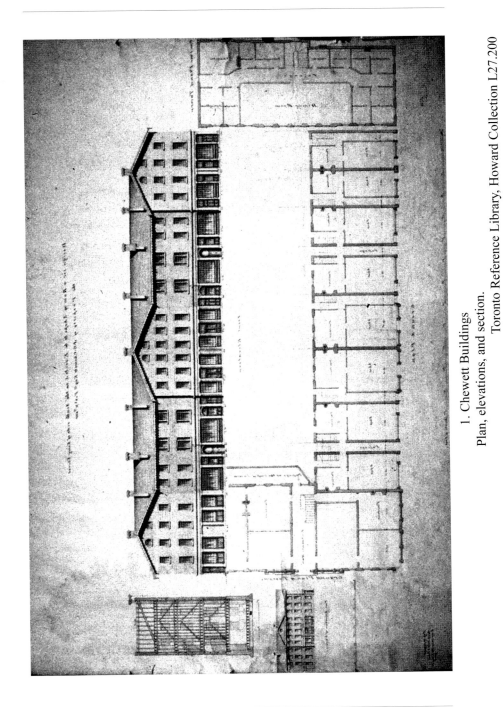

1. Chewett Buildings
Plan, elevations, and section.
Toronto Reference Library, Howard Collection L27.200

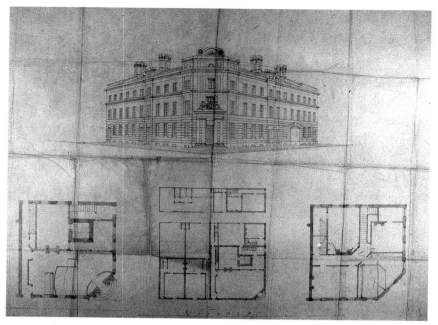

2. Bank of British North America.
Plan and perspective drawing.
Toronto Reference Library, Howard Collection L27.239

Banking institutions joined his clientele in the 1840s. The Roman Doric portico that he added to the Bank of Upper Canada remains a striking feature on Adelaide Street. His Bank of British North America, begun in 1845 at the northeast corner of Yonge and Wellington Streets was much admired for its corner entrance and Ionic portico. The treatment of the upper storey reflects his high regard for the English architect, Sir John Soane.[7] Howard made even further impact on the immediate neighbourhood with adjoining warehouses and other commercial buildings on Wellington.

His residential practice consisted of labourers' cottages, row houses, and suburban villas. His own home, a stuccoed Regency -style cottage, was built in 1837 as a small house that over the years evolved into a two-storey dwelling.[8] Known as Colborne

4. 'Trafalgar Lodge', Trafalgar Avenue, Montreal.
A fine example of residential Gothic Revival.
Photograph ca. 1872; permission of McCord Museum, MP-1984.107.62

Lodge, it is now open to the public. Its spacious drawing room faces south with casement doors opening out onto a wide verandah with a view of Lake Ontario beyond. A trio of chimneys emphasizes the symmetry of the composition.

To Kearnsey House, built in 1844-45 of red brick for William Proudfoot, President of the Bank of Upper Canada, Howard devoted more time and effort than to any other similar commission.[9] Deeply curved bays defined the dining room and boudoir located to either side of a long drawing room. On the exterior he indulged in a lively mix of detail including classical columns, Italianate window heads and chimneys, and decorative treillage.

He occasionally incorporated Gothic Revival detail into his residential work. Albert Furniss probably requested the style for his Montreal dwelling Trafalgar Lodge, built in 1848 and still standing, though a divided residence.[10] With its asymmetrical plan, steeply pitched roof and dormers, lacy bargeboards, and an abundance of interior Gothic mouldings, it exemplifies the picturesque villa. Almost all Howard's churches were built for Anglican congregations between 1841 and 1844 and reflect the early stage of Gothic Revival church design in Ontario, before a more academic approach imposed itself. In general they are built of brick, rectangular in plan with a low-pitched roof, and an entrance through the base of the tower. Internally they are hall-like with the sanctuary projecting into the space, and galleried.[11] Many can still be visited.

In 1841 he built his only Toronto church, the Church of England's first St. Paul's. He was so pleased with his ingenious method of raising its spire that he published an account of it in the *Church*, 21 August 1841. He subdued the engaging blend of classical and Gothic detail used at Holy Trinity, Chippewa, in his designs for churches at Dundas and Holland Landing as well as for St. John's, York Mills, and the sturdy Christ Church, built of stone for the Mohawks of Tyendinaga Township. As noted by

Harold Kalman he introduced the Gothic Revival into Canadian collegiate architecture with his restrained composition for Bishop's College in Lennoxville, Quebec, completed in 1846.[12]

St James' Cemetery set a precedent in local cemetery layout when it was consecrated in 1845. It still offers a pleasurable retreat. For its sixty–five acres located at the edge of Rosedale Ravine, then at Toronto's outskirts, he followed the principles of picturesque planning that had come into vogue for rural cemeteries elsewhere. His arrangement of winding roads relates to the contours of the irregular terrain while enclosing more regular divisions.[13]

5. St John's, York Mills Anglican church, Don Ridge Drive, York Mills.
Toronto Reference Library: T 10764

115

Competition Entries

As did others then and since, Howard entered architectural competitions as a means of gaining recognition and sometimes commissions. In 1837 he won the premium for the design of the London District jail and although the project was set aside, he was quick to publicize his success in March issues of the *Toronto Patriot*. The same year he won the competition for the Home District's Toronto Courthouse and jail. Only the jail was built and even then, only two of three radiating wings. He enriched the modest Palladianism of the Toronto proposal for Brockville's combined courthouse and jail, completed in 1844. With its pedimented centrepiece of raised Ionic columns, it still dominates Brockville's Courthouse Square.[14]

When in June of 1840 Howard won the premium for the design of the Provincial Lunatic Asylum his appointment as architect seemed assured. But the project lagged, partly because of the government's preoccupation with a temporary asylum that was immediately needed. Meanwhile, other architects had opened offices in the city and Howard worried that his winning the premium might, in fact, not guarantee the commission. In a state of acute anxiety he petitioned the Governor General for confirmation of his appointment as architect backing his plea with testimonials.[15] The decision was left to the commissioners who were to oversee the project. Happily, Dr. Christopher Widmer and James G. Chewett, two of Howard's earliest clients, were members of the commission and, with their urging, in December 1844 Howard was named architect.[16]

The government of the Province of Upper Canada had passed an Act in May 1839 authorizing the erection of an Asylum.[17] The selection of the site was the first consideration — was it to be Kingston or Toronto? Ultimately the British government granted the province fifty acres on the Garrison Reserve, about three miles west of Toronto. This met the requirements of the military who

6. Home District Court House and Jail.

Drawing dates from 1836. The jail was completed in 1840 on Front Street east, south side, between Berkeley and Parliament Streets. The windmill at the foot of Trinity Street was built for the Gooderham & Worts distillery in 1832, and was also 'in constant use indicating the basal point for Toronto harbour measurements.'[28]

Toronto Reference Library: T 11968

7A. North View.

The lithograph has been developed from Howard's perspective drawing, discussed in the chapter 'Building Canada West.' It is mentioned in Howard's journal, 10 February and 28 September 1846. Scobie & Balfour, publishers.

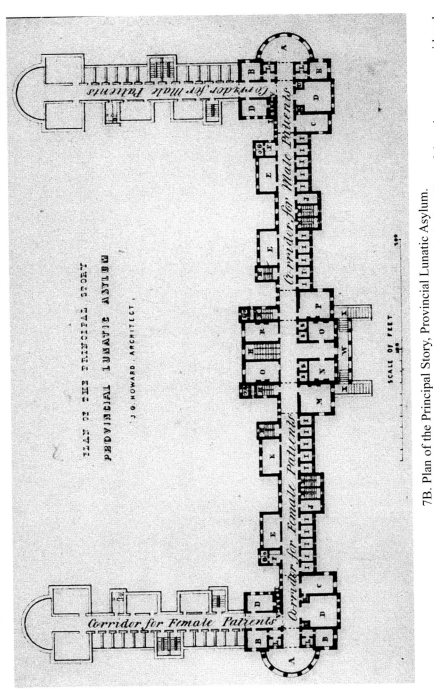

7B. Plan of the Principal Story, Provincial Lunatic Asylum.

This engraving was published by Scobie & Balfour in 1847, and shows how early the building of the wings was considered doubtful. These two pages are an indisputable record of Howard's good business sense in publicizing the building form.

foresaw that the building might be strategically useful should hostilities with the Americans reopen.[18]

The commission's advertisement of the competition (*Toronto Patriot*, 24 April 1840) stated that the asylum was to be constructed of brick, covered with tin, and that it should accommodate two hundred and fifty patients. When its members met on 7 December 1844, after Howard had already begun to rework his design, they decided on the white (buff) brick that he had first used for the Toronto jail and they were prepared to 'allow of stone for the basement above ground, and also for the Lintels and Pilasters & in such proportions as would not materially add to the expense of the erection.'

Work on the Asylum Contract

The following spring, in compliance with the colonial secretary's orders, Howard and two of the commissioners journeyed to Montreal to present the completed plans to the commanding officer of the Royal Engineers who might wish to make suggestions with respect to 'the disposition of the Buildings as may tend to afford collateral defences in the event of it becoming desirable to occupy it hereafter by a local force.' Whether changes were requested is not known, only that the authorities granted approval in June.[19]

With this out of the way, he began intensive work on the project (juggling it with other jobs that were crowding his time). The commissioners' occasional requests for modifications and the consolidation of space culminated in February 1846 in new instructions to plan for three hundred to four hundred patients with the possibility of enlargement at some future date without 'derangement of the plan or unnecessary expense.' But the nervous government still insisted on a substantial reduction in costs. In the next few months Howard scrimped to lop almost nine thousand pounds from his original estimate of fifty thousand pounds.[20] Eventually, on 22 August 1846 with due pomp and ceremony and every stratum of society represented, Chief Justice John Beverley Robinson laid the cornerstone of the building that promised 'health, comfort, security and restoration.'[21]

Despite having to await the Ordnance Department's ongoing and generally grudging approval of such necessities as the construction of a pump house and the main sewer (installed in 1848 with the city's consent), the work proceeded at a satisfactory pace.[22] The red backing brick for the interior walls was made on site; other materials were hauled across the reserve by rail from the pier at the lake shore. Howard was paid three hundred pounds a year for superintending construction.[23] By 8 January 1848 he could report that the project had gone forward 'far beyond my most sanguine expectations.' The brick walls were finished, the dome was in place, nearly all sashes and frames were fixed and glazed, and the tinsmiths already at work on the roof. He worried that the stone portico might be 'overlooked' and was willing to

8. The Spiral staircase.

Under the dome there was a spiral staircase, constructed round an inverted newell post that suspended the staircase from the central opening of the lantern on the dome's summit. The staircase was connected with the perimeter of the dome room via a steep ramp, shown on lower left.

The dynamics of an apparent helical vortex, seemed to hold the structure in mid-air, high above the 12,000 gallon water tank that filled the lower half of the room.

Tradition has it that access to the lantern room was a military requirement. They may have wanted a sentry lookout against invasion, or a beacon for shipping on Lake Ontario.

Reproduced by permission
CAMH, AHCP&MHS

121

8. The entrance gate to Colborne Lodge (upper right).

In 1854 Howard sold a strip of land fronting his property to the Great Western Railway Company, hence the level crossing.

Watercolour on paper, John George Howard, 1855-65.

From the collection of the City of Toronto, Colborn Lodge, John George Howard's Hou...

substitute columns and entablature of wood 'rather than leave the building in an unfinished state.'24 In December 1849 — the facade lacking its stately portico and without the southward-extending wings — the first patients were admitted. The asylum officially opened the following January. The *Globe* judged it to be 'exceedingly handsome, commodious, healthful and safe.' Despite the pleas of the commissioners for the work to be continued, the government held off. Howard attended to unfinished details, wrote reports, and oversaw minor improvements, but his involvement with the building dwindled and by 1853 had ended.

Career Summary

Howard's extant plans, drawings and journals — a voluminous collection — give a picture of his successful working life, outside interests and social activities. He shunned partnership, relying on clerks, apprentices, and very often his wife, for assistance. To complement his practice he became a land agent and notary.25 He acquired properties from which he sold timber and where he built lime kilns and brick works. He was thus positioned to negotiate a client's land purchase, design his building, supply construction materials, and follow through with the sale of the building or the collection of rent. Few architects of the period so fully applied the principle of vertical integration to the enhancement of a practice.

Retirement

Parallel to his energetic hurrying from office to site, he devoted himself to developing the one hundred-and-sixty acre farm west of the city, purchased in 1836, and where he built Colborne Lodge. Although for a time the Howards relocated in Toronto, the farm became their permanent home in 1856 when he retired. There they enjoyed gardening, sketching, and boating on nearby Grenadier Pond. In 1873 he arranged for his property, by then known as High Park, to be conveyed to the city 'as a public park forever.'

Howard enthusiastically involved himself in local cultural life. He was a founder of the artists' societies organized in 1834, and in the 1840s.[26] To their exhibitions he contributed paintings and drawings of ambitious architectural schemes. He was also active in the Mechanics' Institute and was a parishioner of St. James' Anglican Cathedral. Shortly after joining St. Andrew's Masonic Lodge, he incorporated its new quarters into his plan for Beard's Hotel, built at the corner of Church and Colborne Streets in 1847.

While his journals and correspondence reveal an independent man, impatient to get ahead, he seems to have been thought of as kind-hearted and often generous. In the course of his childless marriage to Jemima, he formed a liaison with a Toronto woman, Mary Williams, who bore him three children. Whatever shadow this may have cast on his marriage he retrospectively described it as 'singularly happy' and seems genuinely to have mourned Jemima's death in 1877.[27] He designed the monument that marks their graves near their home and when he died in 1890 the Toronto *Mail* (7 February) commented that 'the number of representative and influential men' who gathered for the funeral service at Colborne Lodge demonstrated in what 'high esteem he was held and how deeply his public munificence was appreciated.'

. SIX .

JOSEPH WORKMAN
ASYLUM SUPERINTENDENT

by Christine I. M. Johnston

DR JOSEPH WORKMAN is 'thick-skinned,' and an 'irascible, implacable despot.' In 1857 these severe words were written by George Brown in the Globe, the largest newspaper of its day in Canada West[1]. Workman was the Superintendent of the Provincial Asylum. Yet in 1980 when the new concrete Auditorium was added to the front of the Administration Building it was named in Workman's honour, and a bust of Joseph greets you in a case at the front entrance. Indeed at the official opening, a staff member dressed up as the good doctor and read one of his speeches. These two divergent perceptions show the challenges and controversies surrounding Workman, as during his twenty-two years in office (1853 to 1875), he established the framework not only for the Toronto institution but for all doctors working in Canadian asylums. Often he is called the Father of Canadian Psychiatry.[2]

Workman was the second Superintendent of Howard's Toronto Asylum, and his pioneer role has long been recognized. The choice of Workman for Superintendent was a mixture of good judgment and patronage. In 1853, Dr. John Rolph, a key figure in the national government, proposed his friend be made Interim Superintendent, giving Workman the opportunity to display his skills. There was stiff competition for the permanent job, which Workman won a year later. Workman's position was helped by legislation introduced by Rolph in 1853 which gave the Superintendent new powers to control staffing and finances (with the exception of firing the Bursar). Previously there had been many inappropriate patronage appointments amongst the general staff.

1. Dr. Joseph Workman.

Reproduced by permission CAMH, AHCP&MHS

Workman had qualified as a doctor in Montreal, and at the time of his appointment was an occasional teacher in Rolph's School of Medicine. He first come to Toronto to manage the family hardware business and was a well-known political figure in the city. He had: co-founded the Toronto Board of Trade; been elected to a term as Alderman and later the School Board, where he was the first Chairman; been a key writer of the Royal Commission report which helped establish the secular University College in Toronto. Workman's name was synonymous with some truly scathing newspaper editorials and as an orator he freely used sarcasm, irony and even ridicule to demolish his opponents. Yet to his allies he personified integrity, stability and kindness.

Workman was new to managing a big institution, and in order to learn quickly, took an extended tour of institutions here and abroad in 1854-55. Upon his return he began staff training, attempted to tighten up administrative systems and took advantage of the new Act to fire and hire staff. Despite good intentions, in 1856 crises arose. First he got into a power struggle with the Bursar and began communicating with him only through notes. As a result of the conflict, Workman spent time needlessly planning the purchases and not supervising or managing properly. Next, a former porter named Magar accused the Steward of inadequately protecting female patients from the sexual advances of a male patient. In addition, Magar reported that an unruly female patient had been placed in a straight jacket and left alone in a "place of punishment" where she unexpectedly gave birth. Workman, her physician, denied knowledge of her pregnancy[3]. An official inquiry by the Visiting Commissioners cleared Workman and it might have all ended there. But fifteen years prior, Workman had written controversial editorials for the *Mirror*, a rival of the *Globe*. Without comment, Brown now printed Magar's allegations, which included a personal vilification of Workman. The situation escalated and neither man backed down.

Workman was called 'tyrannical, controlling and conceited', as well as an 'irascible, implacable despot.' Finally, Workman sued Brown for libel. At the trial ten of the jury voted for Brown and only two for Workman. The Attorney General in Canada West, Sir John A. Macdonald, felt obliged to make sure the name of the public appointee was clear. Magar was charged by the Crown with libel. A second trial followed closely on the first, with Brown openly assisting Magar. Again the libel charges failed, but this time the crown paid the bill. Interestingly, William Lyon Mackenzie chose not to print one word of the conflict in his paper. Surprising, because a few weeks before he had raged at Workman over his daughter, who was a patient in the Asylum. In addition, he had unsuccessfully tried to persuade Workman to withdraw the libel suit.[4]

Workman set about establishing proceedures to improve the management within the institution. Over time he built a reputation for fighting for the rights of his patients and staff. He declared that it was the moral duty of the Superintendent to defend the staff from unjust accusations.

Workman argued repeatedly and vociferously for more space, arguing that mental patients needed more air than other patients, and that if the Asylum was to be curative rather than merely custodial, then a complete system of classification within the Asylum had to be in effect. So Workman insisted that the wings to Howard's building should be added. Institutional space was found elsewhere for the criminally insane, the gentle incurables, and the mentally challenged (the authour's politically correct term).

Much of the program Workman implemented at the Asylum was not original. Rather he strove to implement in Canada the European 'moral treatment' then advocated by pioneers like Pinel and the Tuke brothers. Hallmarks of it were kindness, good food, exercise, fresh air, good medical care, and something akin to occupational therapy. Workman also introduced group work, and the concept of outpatients and the occasional 'halfway house'. Entertainment was brought in and of course religious services. He organized a library and brought in daily newspapers (except the *Globe!*).

Restraints, in common use at that time, he discouraged unless the safety of the staff was at stake. He used alcohol and opium to sedate the patients instead of all the heavy medications previously used. This merited some severe criticism in the *Globe!*

Workman performed autopsies (and a few illegal dissections) because he thought that patients had a physical predisposition to madness, triggered by an event, accident or illness, which had formerly been called the 'causes.' This was of course before the days of biochemistry, so Workman searched in vain for the physical cause. His comment in later years was:

> The advancement of sound pathological science, in the present day, depends perhaps more on the careful consideration, and proper application, of existing simple facts, than on the discovery of additional or complex ones. We may spend much time in search of great truths which ultimately we may find have all the while been at our fingers.[5]

He stressed the importance of taking family histories, seeking hereditary traits, because he was aware that many patients seemed to be born with a tendency to mental illness. He observed dysfunctional families but saw the illness as the cause and not the result of the family dynamics. Freud, Jung and psychoanalysis had not yet arrived on the scene. He studied alcoholism and even noted what we now call 'fetal alcohol syndrome.'

At Workman's suggestion, the study of alienism (now known as psychiatry) was introduced into medical schools in the U.S.A. and Ontario. The concept of internships or residents-in- training was his original idea. The Government allowed him to introduce it at the Asylum but discontinued it when he retired. In this program he launched the careers of several famous psychiatrists. Charles K. Clarke began his apprenticeship with Workman when only sixteen years old. Many years later he wrote to his mentor:

> You have not lived in vain. Those of us who love you best would express the admiration we feel. There are few of us perhaps who fully understand what your influence has been on Asylum management in Ontario. I know that in my work the precepts and examples laid down by you, come home to me with peculiar force almost every hour, and when I allow them to act as guiding stars, I never go astray. Those of us still alive, are, as a unit in our regard for the good old man who has been a father to them.[6]

Workman inspired many. Some of his advice, given to medical students in 1880 is as follows:

> It is too easy to forget that the ends we serve is not our careers, to rise in our profession and receive accolades from our peers, but humanity. If we are no better than pedlars seeking profit, albeit in honours not dollars, then we should leave medicine. The easiest thing to do is to lock the insane in cells and feed them and forget them. The hardest is to find that spark of humanity that dwells in each of us. We are all tempted to quit the race at one time or another. But, as was said so very long ago, the race is not to the swift. No, it is to he who perseveres. I pass the torch to you.[7]

At aged seventy, Workman officially retired. Honours were heaped on him from the U.S.A., Great Britain and Italy as well as from his country of adoption, Canada. He also played a leadership role in the professional organizations he helped to found, acting as the first president of both the Ontario Medical Association and the Toronto Medical Society. He had helped establish the Canadian Medical Association back in 1867, and ten years later took on the

Presidency. Some accused him of being vain and arrogant, and certainly he 'was a man of vigour, of wit, and possessed of a well-sharpened and well- trained pen, and attacked quite as successfully as he resisted.'[8] But he would not have lasted for twenty-two years as head of the Asylum if he had not been tough as well as enlightened and humane.

2. Tully/Workman Wing.

Reproduced by permission CAMH, AHCP&MHS

. SEVEN .

HOWARD vs. TULLY
CONTRAST & COMPARISON

by Steven Bell

To relate to our fellow creatures, we reveal something of our true selves. Some of us are effusive, others taciturn. We seldom expose all aspects of ourselves and this may even make us more intriguing to others, suggesting that there is something to be discovered. Similarly, a building may initially express its nature and function only in part, and await further exploration before revealing its full significance. A building has many things to say.

Harry Mayerovich 'How Architecture Speaks...and fashions our lives'

THE PURPOSE OF THIS PAPER is to provide an architectural overview and comparison of the design for the east and west wings of the historic Provincial Lunatic Asylum at Toronto, contrasting John George Howard's proposed 1844-1845 design with the as-built 1866-70 design by Kivas Tully, Architect under the direction of Dr Joseph Workman.

Historical & Architectural Background

John Howard's design for the Provincial Lunatic Asylum is modeled after the National Gallery on Trafalgar Square in London by William Wilkens. The National Gallery was constructed in the Neo-Classical style, a style that set out to return 'order' to society, and which emerged in response to the flamboyant architecture of the high Renaissance, otherwise known as the Baroque and

Rococo (1600-1780). Neo-Classicism, also referred to as the 'architecture of reason', grew out of the intellectual movement of the Enlightenment developed within the rigid system of rule known as 'absolutism'. Transcending Europe, North America and other parts of the world, it was believed that Neo-Classicism, through the built environment, could be used to have a positive influence on the spirit of the people and inspire them to behave in a manner based on reason and morality. The Neo-Classic style arrived in Upper Canada in the first quarter of the 19th century and was adopted by John Howard as the style of choice for constructing the first Provincial Lunatic Asylum.

1. North elevation of the Provincial Lunatic Asylum(above)
and South elevation (below).
Shaded drawing by John Howard circa 1845, before construction began.
Toronto Reference Library 423a 916 (part)

In terms of built-form, the design of the Provincial Lunatic Asylum was configured to have a main edifice measuring some 584 feet in length with a north orientation to Queen Street and two large wings positioned on the south side at right angles to form a quadrangle. Functionally, the wings were intended to provide accommodation for the 'most-excited' and mentally challenged class of patients. Architecturally, they were designed to have the same form and Neo-Classic expression as the main block of the hospital.

The rationale infused into the planning of Howard's Asylum was greatly compromised when the provincial government decided to only construct the main block of the hospital in 1846. However, in response to a growing population and severe overcrowding conditions two decades later, the asylum was expanded with the addition of the east and west wings. Rather than build the wings according to the plans prepared by John Howard, Kivas Tully, a prominent 19th century Toronto architect, was commissioned to redesign and oversee their construction based on sketches made by the Medical Superintendent Workman. The wings were started in 1866 and completed in 1869.

John Howard's Design for the Provincial Lunatic Asylum

The organizing principles in the design of Howard's asylum complex are based on ordered arrangements, strong axial symmetry, a repetition of forms, clear expression of function, and a well defined spatial and volumetric hierarchy. The approach to the design can be described as follows:

The principle entrance, administration offices, and public reception areas represent the centre of authority of the asylum and are expressed as the critical mass within the entire scheme. This pavilion is positioned centrally and is the focus of the front (north) elevation. Extending off to the sides of the centre pavilion, are the two arms of the asylum — one dedicated to the care of male patients and the other for female patients. Common, leisure and passive spaces are placed at the extremes of the arms and read as secondary pavilions according to their form and architectural expression. These spaces have 'outward' looking views onto the

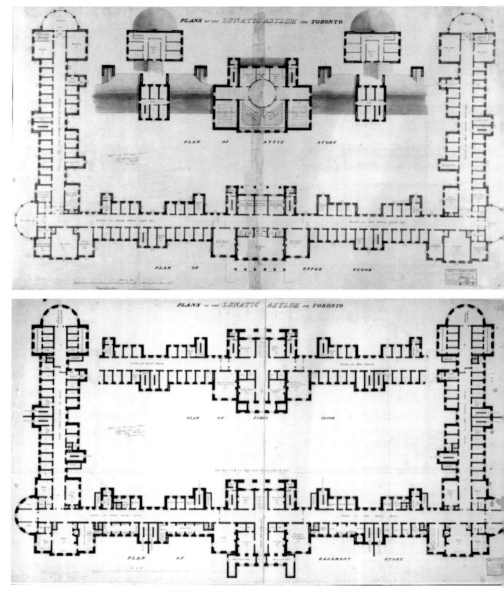

2. Plans for the Lunatic Asylum in Toronto.
These are the project drawings for all four floors, signed and dated 1845.

neighbouring grounds. Patient rooms are located between the common spaces and the central administration pavilion. In these areas, dormitories face south (towards Lake Ontario) and private rooms are placed along the north side fronting onto Queen Street. In plan, the arms of the hospital (although linear in nature) are dynamic, lively, and have a sense of rhythm in their interconnecting forms. Vertical circulation is placed at mid-point within each of the arms (and symmetrically distributed on north façade of the Howard block on either side of the central pavilion). A corridor measuring 14 ft wide serves as the principal circulation space and traverses the entire length of the floor plate.

In the design of the wings, Howard proposed the same hierarchy of spaces, allocating principal and public rooms to the extremes of the floor plate and placing patient rooms between common areas. However, on some floors, the southern ends of the wings were designed as self-contained areas for quarantine and isolation of the 'most excited' class of patients.

In terms of room sizes for patient rooms, public spaces and the principle corridor, Howard repeats the same system of dimensions and proportions within the wings. The spatial experience is also identical, incorporating a symmetrical distribution of rooms located on either side of a wide centre hall (also measuring 14 feet), principle vertical circulation located centrally, large airy common rooms at the extremities and a projecting half circle verandah terminating at the ends. At certain locations, windows have been strategically introduced into the wall of the corridor (where the corridor is manipulated in plan to form a part of the external wall) in order to provide direct access to the outside, ventilation and views of the outdoor common space (as defined by the U-shape/quadrangle configuration of the complex). Although, these windows have controlled views, i.e. directed to the opposite sides of the hospital wings, they are repeated in the wings as an architectural treatment also featured in the main block.

3. Kivas Tully.

Born in England in 1820 and emigrated in 1844. Although by some measures
a successful rival, he was helped and encouraged by John Howard.

Photograph
Reproduced by permission of CAMH, AHCP&MHS

Design & Construction of the East & West Wings
by Kivas Tully, Architect

The design of the as-built 1866 wings by Kivas Tully, to some degree reiterates the design principles found in John Howard's original concept for the wings. However, there are several distinctive and subtle differences between the two designs that shed interesting light on the approach used by either architect.

Kivas Tully approached the design of the wings as independent masses to the main hospital building. The wings measured 215 feet in length and were 60 feet wide. Vertically, they projected four storeys in height and had 12 ft interior ceiling heights. Access to the wings from the main hospital was provided by a narrow physical link (one at each wing) at the ground floor level. These connections were frame, measuring 30 x 9 ft. They were said to be designed to control the spread of fire between buildings. Moreover, the most severely disturbed patients under the care of the asylum could be quarantined in the wings.

In plan, Tully's design for the wings is significantly compressed, spatially rigid, and incorporates an efficient functional building program. Similarly, it emulates the spatial organization and sequence of rooms as proposed by Howard in his initial plans, i.e. common areas, such as sitting rooms are allocated to the extremes of the wings, vertical circulation and attendants rooms at the centre(s), and patient rooms uniformly allocated between these zones. It is interesting to note that in Tully's design, patient rooms are equally distributed on either side of the corridor, whereas Howard put them on one side only. Also Tully's room dimensions are considerably smaller, and the proportions appear to be more oblong, i.e. patient rooms within the wings measured 12 x 6 ft, compared to the more comfortable 12 x 10 ft proportion used by Howard.

The principal corridor, which traverses the length of the wing(s), is also narrower than that of Howard's design and has a

LUNATIC ASYLUM TORONTO

LUNATIC ASYLUM,
TORONTO.

4. Department of Public Works. Report of architect K.Tully, 1869.

re: Lithographs and Engravings of Public Buildings.

As applications have been made continually to the Department for information respecting the dimensions and appearance of the several public buildings now in progress of construction and as it is desirable that full particulars be given to the members of the Legislature respecting same, I recommend that small lithographs and engravings should be prepared and printed with your Report on Public Works. The drawings to comprise perspective views and ground plans of the Lieutenant Governor's Residence, Lunatic Asylum at Toronto and London, and of the Deaf and Dumb Institute at Belleville. A Printed explanation and description of the several buildings will also accompany the engraving.

This method has been accepted and carried out in the United States for several years and has afforded much satisfying information respecting Public Works in that country.   *Kivas Tully*

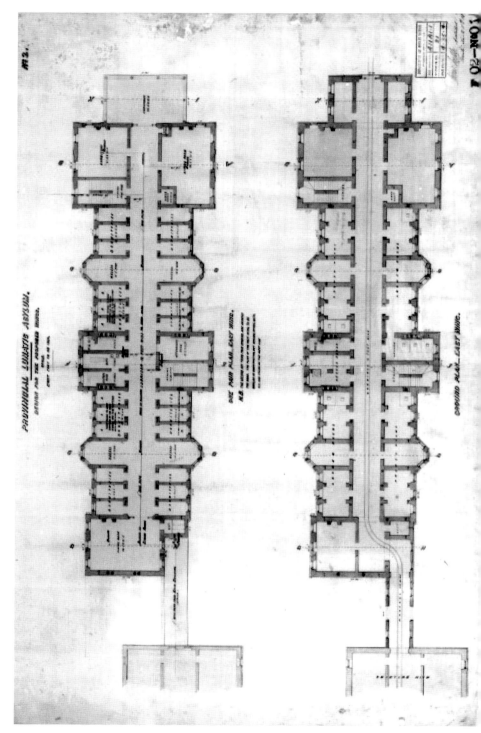

5. Provincial Lunatic Asylum – Design for Proposed Wings, 1868.
Plan drawing by Kivas Tully, blue ink on pink rag paper. Archives of Ontario RG 15-13-2-43

shorter length, and lacks exterior windows that open directly on the hall. This suggests that the corridor may have been considered a purely functional entity, rather than an interactive, enhancing circulatory space as perceived and intended by John Howard. Regardless, even with a narrower width, Tully does not altogether abandon the need to provide 'social opportunities' along the path of circulation. In contrast to Howard's design, Tully incorporates open 'recesses' that appear as transepts across the wings (symmetrically positioned on either side of the centres of the wings) and which break the strong linear character of the corridor system. As a form of 'public' space, the recesses run the full width of the wing, terminating at the exterior walls in the form of bay windows. Their architectural qualities, being somewhat domestic in nature, would have provided a connection to the exterior (albeit limited) through views to the neighbouring grounds. Nonetheless, like the single dormitories, the recesses are spatially restrained in their overall dimensions, measuring only 10 feet across their width.

The concept of the outdoor verandah, projecting from the ends of the wings, is an element that is carried over from the main hospital block and the initial design of the wings by Howard. However, in Tully's design, the verandah takes on a simple rectangular form instead of circular one, but is in keeping with the overall rectilinear character of the wings. In conjunction with their southern orientation, setting and exposure to the Lake, the use of the rectangular verandah may be perceived as having domestic qualities of permanence and sustainability. Geometrically, the rectangle is also a static object and may be used creatively in architecture to express 'order', 'restraint' and 'control'. In contrast, the circular form employed by Howard in the main block evokes a sense of emotion, a dynamic flowing quality, and is visually 'freed' from the plan. Whether because of symbolic, practical, or economical reasons, Tully in his design of

6. View of the Asylum from north west, about 1870.
This early photograph shows the verandah before it was modified. Increasing pressures to provide more and more sleeping accommodation lead to its permanent enclosure in the twentieth century.
Ontario Archives, acc 9569, S-15336 and CAMH, AHCP&MHS

the wings may have felt that the curvilinear form was too overpowering, too ambitious and perhaps not appropriate for accommodating patients of long-term and perpetual care.

Individuality within a free society can only be guaranteed by some system of order. In architecture, variety (to avoid confusion or anarchy) must be contained within an embracing unity. 'Freedom,' said the poet Robert Frost, 'is feeling easy in harness'.

A comparative Analysis of the Wings in Elevation.

During the last half of the 19th century, the introduction of the picturesque, romantic, exotic and eclectic styles in Ontario offered architects and builders a greater choice of styles in which to fashion their buildings. By the 1860s, the Gothic Revival, Italianate, Romanesque Revival, and Second Empire styles came into vogue, and the popularity of the Classical Revival began to decline. Many of these 'romantic' styles lent themselves to the design of large edifices, including commercial buildings and prominent institutions. In the design of the Asylum's wings, Kivas Tully sought to incorporate some of the latest architectural fashions, without compromising the gracious character of Howard's Neo-Classical block.

Although a clear building evolution is easily understood, Tully's design for the elevations of the wings evokes a different reaction when studied against the very formal nature of the Neo-Classical Howard block. In general, the Tully elevations appear more picturesque in character. From a distance, the wings appear as an eclectic assembly of row houses.

In the design of the wings by Tully, the spatial efficiency of the plan, and condensed organization of interior functions is clearly reflected in the elevations. Careful study of the exterior proportions reveals that there is a sense of reduced width in individual bays and projections, giving way to an illusion of greater height in the façade(s). This approach is both consistent and reflective of the architectural trends and proportion systems evolving within the design of buildings constructed in the last half of the 19th century.

In the treatment of the elevations, Tully has not altogether rejected the classical language used in the 1844 Howard block. Interestingly, Tully employs a variety of forms, such as square, rectangular and angular-bay projections, but maintains the sense of balance and symmetry that is distinctly classical.

Although articulated by obvious breaks, the roof is primarily gabled along the length of the wing. Differences occur where the centralized mass containing the stairwells is raised above the roof level by one storey and subsequently given a hipped configuration in order to denote its secondary importance in the overall function and architectural expression of the wing (this approach is similar to Howard's). The addition of parapeted gable walls (a.k.a. fire-walls) at the extremes of the wings form pavilion-like masses and serve to break the horizontal emphasis of the entire elevation. They also describe the function of interior spaces at these respective locations, i.e. day rooms, common areas, etc.

Despite the vertical emphasis of the elevations, Tully has maintained the same sense of scale, and sequence of masonry wall treatments in the design of the wings by using a two-storey base supporting the upper two storeys and the articulation of the masonry wall using pilasters and projecting belt courses. Although the form and massing of the wing appears to be quite varied, there is a sense of regularity and uniformity within the design on account of the 3-ranked window arrangements which are used throughout.

The projecting bay windows, which rise 4 storeys in height along the exterior walls, are clearly an eclectic injection of the 1860s. As an early architectural invention of the Gothic style, bay windows appeared as a feature in domestic architecture of Ontario during the 19th century. The use of this feature, as applied to a long-term care institution, comments on Tully's interpretation of the building program and the 'domestic' image he wanted to communicate to the public intellect.

Superimposed on the roof of the wings, and axially in-line with the bay windows, are two sets of cupolas (one set to each wing). Visually, the cupolas reinforce the presence of the bay windows on the elevations, and second, make the visual connection to the larger dome on the Howard block. Their presence also

7. Tully East Wing.
Photographed in 1950s from the dome of the Howard building. The grass
quadrangle shows in the foreground.
Photographer: Roy Essex (staff)
Reproduced by permission CAMH, AHCP&MHS

provides a sense of architectural unity for the entire asylum complex.

Despite a twenty-year time difference between the erection of the Howard block and the Kivas Tully wings, a large degree of unity and continuity exists in the detailing of the overall complex. In terms of the 1866 wings, this is evident in the configuration of apertures with their simplified Greek-inspired stone surrounds, the streamline classical treatment around the eaves and the overall incorporation of classical language and the symmetrical approach to the design. In effect, there is a successful translation of architectural form between historical periods, but a differing system of values is noted when comparing the designs of Howard to those of Tully.

For a contemporary assessment of the building when completed we turn to the report by the Provincial Inspector J. W. Langmuir

> The condition of the Asylum with respect to cleanliness and order was most excellent. The dormitories, and the beds... The wards and sitting-rooms are very comfortable and in the new wings and the hospitals are even very cheerful but it appears most desirable to increase...the means of interesting and amusing the patients, the want of occupation...must have a very depressing effect which cannot but hinder and retard cures...It must be admitted however that there are serious difficulties in the way of overcoming this drawback owing chiefly to the solitary and melancholy habits of a large portion of the insane...This is the most marked structural defect .

The differences between the Howard and the Tully designs can be interpreted as a change not only in architectural taste, but also a change in social values, attitudes and practices in the treatment of the mentally challenged during the last half of the 19th century.

. EIGHT .

Dr.DANIEL CLARK: ASYLUM SUPERINTENDENT

by Alec Keefer

...we stop before a door on the left of the entrance hall bearing the words: **Superintendent: private**. Here visitors whose friends are within the building come for the news...joy that the loved one will soon be restored or sorrow...Many a sad word is spoken here and many a comforting one, for Dr. Clark is a kindly man, whose experience instead of hardening has made him all the more tender ...We knock and are invited in. The Superintendent is a stout, medium sized gentleman, a little past middle age,...there is indication of great humour and "pawkiness" in the keen eyes...The Doctor talks freely of the Asylum, its position, relative importance and efficiency. He tells us that the Toronto Asylum while a great institution with 710 patients..., is far distanced by the Willard of New York with over 2000...the doctor speaks of improvements in the method of treating the insane. This is a topic of which as he himself puts it, he is full. In *"Half Hours in an Asylum"* written for....*Canadian Monthly* he has dealt with the subject fully.

The Saturday Globe, 5 April 1890.

ALTHOUGH THE SELECTION OF DR DANIEL CLARK in 1875 to be Superintendent of the Provincial Lunatic Asylum broke with the established protocol, Clark was held in such high regard by his colleagues that it was selection by acclamation. For he was anything but the rural general practitioner he appeared. His reputation

1. Dr. Daniel Clark.

Reproduced by permission CAMH, AHCP&MHS

as the Asylum's Physician was so high that it was to Clark that the legal defence turned to in 1885 as an expert witness on insanity at the trial of Louis Riel. After interviewing Riel at length, and studying related correspondence and other documents, Clark was confident in diagnosing Riel as a shrewd and intelligent man who suffered from bouts of insanity. However the Court chose, unwisely, to overlook his skilful and reasoned interpretation of that situation and did not grant the clemency that Clark had argued was the proper response.

By all accounts Clark was a grand original: authority on the treatment of mental disorders, literary critic, raconteur and novelist. His life up until his appointment had been a classic, Horatio Alger story filled with daring-do and fantastic exploits as far a field as the California gold rush. But in the end the most important and lasting achievement would be his 'improvements' to the Provincial Lunatic Asylum.

By the scope of his actions and habits of mind, we readily see that he arrived knowing full well that heroic gestures and vitriolic prose were not about to motivate the Provincial Legislature to do what should be done for the good of the residents of the Asylum. Ever the tireless optimist, while he clearly did have major long term goals with regard to the nature of the space in which he wanted to house and heal his patients, he prudently moved forward by incremental staged projects. Only when we retrace the path he took, over his three decade tenure, do we realize how significant were his achievements.

And what of this institution that Daniel was about to invest with 30 years of his life? Workman said of it:

> visitors to this Asylum seldom fail to admire its architectural beauty and amplitude of its dimensions ... [And as] to architectural device, excellence of workmanship and the general suitableness of its interior arrangement, this Toronto Asylum is inferior to none other on the continent.

2. Superintendent's House.
Completed in 1878, this house stood until the building program of the 1970's.
This is where Daniel Clark and his family lived during his entire term as
Superintendent. Then in the twentieth century, as the requirement for the
Superintendent to live on the premises was abandoned, the house was used as
a nurses' residence for a number of years.

Architects: John Palmer, George Harding
Glass negative (H)
Reproduced by permission CAMH, AHCP&MHS

Clark's response in 1875 to his new employment situation
was expressed in broad magisterial terms:

Much has been done for the best by my distinguished predecessor during his administration of twenty-three years but
progression is always demanded and will be in the future as
well as in the past until perfection is reached.

In most cases his progress — physical changes and improvements — Clark realized would of necessity be achieved in partnership with others. First in importance, would be building and maintaining rapport with the Provincial Inspectors, men such as J.W. Langmuir. Equally important would be the staff in the Department Public Works, men like Architect Kivas Tully. For all the plans and specifications for the projects, would originate with them. Also important, especially with very large undertakings, was the free labour provided by prisoners from the new Central Prison on Strachan Avenue. A unique example was the 1881 slaughter house that was put up on the far side of the south wall. This facility was shared jointly with the Andrew Mercer Reformatory for women, just west Asylum on King Street and with the Central Prison who had supplied the heavy manual labour.

When Clark arrived the quadrangle was dominated by sheds, lean-tos and containers to store all materials entering or leaving the building. It had proved impossible to keep the yard in order and clean so three new sheds were erected along the south wall. Ever the poet, Clark had one built of stone; one of brick; and, one of wood. Then he had the quadrangle resodded and a flower garden planted. A bowling green and grounds for croquet were laid out. There was even room for an 'airing court under the trees for (less active) patients.'

Within two years of his arrival Clark had convinced Inspector J. W. Langmuir to obtain funds to build a home for the Superintendent near Queen Street to the east of the East lodge. This freed up rooms in the main building for more patients. In 1875 all the food was prepared in four kitchens and a bakery in the basement. Clark found that the 'odours from these permeated all parts of the building and were at times far from being perfumes.' In 1887 he set to work and erected a new kitchen and bakery along the south wall attached to the laundry south of the central building. It was 110 feet by 33 feet and two stories tall. The

3. East Lodge.
There were two lodge houses built in 1850, one for the engineer and this one for the grounds keeper of the asylum. The design carried forward the noble vision of the main building. The mansard roofs were added in 1886, increasing the comfort of the accomodation for a family. The rear brick wall of the asylum conservatory (greenhouse) can be seen beyond the lodge.

Photograph about 1910
Reproduced by permission CAMH, AHCP&MHS

second story was used as bedrooms for the women who ran the kitchen and laundry.

In 1888 fire escapes of wrought iron were installed throughout the main building, by the patentee himself, Mr Batten. After, the Superintendent offered that all had 'an additional sense of security.' In that same year the one storey wooden halls that connected the Tully/Workman wings with the Howard building were replaced with more substantial brick and stone three-storey versions.

An important project that took eight years to achieve was building, in the forty-five foot space beside the connecting corridors of three stories between the main building and the Tully/Workman wings. The plans and specifications for these infirmaries were ready in 1888. But the male in the west wing was completed until 1893 and the female, in the east wing would wait until 1895. These infirmaries took the place of the Tully free standing hospitals, which had been built in 1866.

Clark reported that of the twelve dining-rooms, six in the Howard and three each in the Tully/Workman wings none, had either sculleries nor pantries. So he was forced 'to partition off rooms in connection with each.' While indeed, the plan of the two wings shows that none were provided, that was not the case in the Howard where originally space was provided. Earlier re-workings under Workman must have removed them or changed their use.

Housing the ever-growing population at the Asylum was a struggle. To free up more space Clark moved the shop of the carpenters and engineers to a two-storey brick building he had constructed along the south wall just west of the laundry. 100 feet by 30 feet, it also accommodated the blacksmith's forge and painter's shop. Clark reported with pride that 25 more patients found beds.

He addressed the need for occupational work, (especially for those in the Tully/Workman wings,) by constructing an addition, 65 feet by 40 feet, just south of the central building. The top floor had a public hall with a seating capacity of 300. Below was a general activity room for the patient's workshops; boots and shoes were made, as was tinware. Space was found for a broad range of works; upholstering, bookbinding, and general repair jobs. 1903 saw the construction of the gymnasium, bowling proved popular.

A number of years ago twenty-five acres of our fifty acres were taken away from us. As the brick wall had to be taken down we were obliged to re-build part of it ourselves around the new boundaries at both ends of our present enclosure. This was extensive work as we had to take down the old wall and use old bricks in the new erection. There were seven hundred and twenty yards of wall built and with the foundations averaged at least sixteen feet in height. As might be expected a number of minor changes in structure have been accomplished by our people. These are such as the building of baths, the reconstructing of the verandahs, the making of a new main entrance instead of the former one into the basement, the building of a new dry-goods store, the re-arranging of the old kitchen into grocery store, the rebuilding of the mortuary, the reconstructing of our conservatory.

4. Lawn Bowling.
A tournament in the quadrangle, about 1910.

Glass negative (K)
Reproduced by permission CAMH, AHCP&MHS

5. Addition to the Central building (above), asylum workshop (below left),
the public hall decorated for Christmas (right).
Reproduced by permission CAMH, AHCP&MHS and Archives of Ontario

Daniel Clark was forced to retire in 1905 due to failing health. He lingered until 1912, but still his passing was the subject of much public grief. The contemporary professional assessment was fulsome:

It is interesting to note that over 5,000 cases came under his care in the thirty years of his incumbency and over 2,000 have recovered and 1,000 improved. The high character of the Institution has been maintained ... and no slander or mal-administration has occurred in connection with its difficult executive work. We take to ourselves credit for the erection of these many structures by the faithful and intelligent work of our patients and their attendants.

One of Daniel Clark's successors H. Clare wrote in 1927 that:

While this institution is old, its features now compare very favourably with those observed in institutions constructed in recent years.

Another successor W. Ross concurred four years later.:

I am pleased to say that throughout the year the work of the Hospital has gone on with the greatest harmony ... staff doing his or her work most cheerfully and conscientiously.

In Daniel Clark the institution found an administrator with the breadth of vision, determination and energy to realize some of the potential of the Toronto Asylum.

WILLIAM JAMES THOMSON (Guelph 1858 - Toronto 1927) may have painted this large but apparently unsigned watercolour (shown on previous page) now at the Centre for Adiction & Mental Health Archives. (Thomson was staff artist of the Toronto *Globe* in the late 1880s and early '90s, and founding president of the Society of Canadian Painters-Etchers.) The extraordinary aerial view creatively offers a prospect of the complex building similar to what one would see if, anchored in a balloon above Queen Street just west of Ossington Street, and looking southeasterly toward Lake Ontario. Thomson prepared a pen-and-ink sketch (now in Ontario Archives), based on this watercolour, for the illustration that accompanies the following text from an informative full-page account of a visit 'At the Asylum', *The Saturday Globe*, 5 April 1890, p. 1 [C.B.,A.K.,D.S.R.]

...the great central building, four and five stories in height. with a facade, facing north, of 854 feet, and the dome rising from the centre, [is] the same in appearance as when finished forty years ago. The wings...extend from either end of the main building in a southerly direction, and are 340 feet long....[t]here patients have bedrooms for themselves,...and everything is more home like. To the south, verandahs afford a splendid view of the bay and the lake in the distance....[T]he principal thing that demands attention is the vast extent of the central building. A great front, with cut stone facing and walls of white brick,...and at the end huge verandahs, three storeys high,...a splendid thing when the weather is too stormy to admit of patients going out....In summer there is the exercise to be had in the grounds, where spreading trees and rich coloured flowers and fountains whose waters sparkle in the sun are seen on all hands. There is the orchard and gardens, a never-failing scene of delight.

. NINE .

Dr C. K. CLARKE

AND

THE TRAINING SCHOOL FOR

NURSES

by William H. Brown

A GROUP PORTRAIT IS A SOCIAL DOCUMENT offering the viewer a glimpse, however tentative, into a particular assembly of people and into their social reality. A graduation photograph has both a private and a public meaning. As a private keepsake, the picture serves as a memory of a group of friends and colleagues. But as a public document, the graduation photograph serves to valorize the educational facility that produced the graduates. In the latter context, the individual identity of each subject is subordinated to the group and its emblems of existence.

This group of young women is easily recognized. They are student nurses. Their uniforms, consisting of freshly starched white aprons and caps pinned onto their tresses, are their emblems and give the women their group definition. Their youthful faces with solemn, even wary or beleaguered expressions, engage directly with the camera. A significant event is clearly being remembered in the photograph. The women face the viewer (and hence the future) with a high seriousness that probably made some of them want to giggle. If they had dared!

To the present-day viewer, the young women look a bit like domestic servants or else select members of a religious order. Present-day nurses, particularly the ones who served their apprentice years in the hospital training schools, will find this group portrait instantly recognizable. The picture was taken to celebrate the 'capping ceremony' that originally climaxed the end of the first year of training.[1]

'Capping' was a milestone in the incremental   process of

1. The Capping Ceremony.
Student nurses at the Queen Street training school for nurses, about 1906,
posed on the lawns of the asylum. Probably the first class to pass through.
Glass negative (A)
Reproduced by permission CAMH, AHCP&MHS

nursing schools. It went like this: the student was at first an unini-
tiated novice. Gradually over the course of the first year, she accu-
mulated enough knowledge and experience from working on the
hospital units to assume more independent responsibility.
Working initially under the watchful and mentoring guidance of a
graduate nurse (a 'grad'), the apprentices eventually provided
most of the staffing in the hospital.

The capping ceremony was a rite of passage signaling this
transition. The entire training system was an example of what
might be called benign mutual exploitation: the nurses received
bed, board and a profession at the end of the process while the

hospital was guaranteed a renewable and subservient workforce, at premium rates, to staff their nursing care units. Most important however, the hospital could oversee the professional training of their nursing staff to ensure that certain standards were met.

Present-day nurses will also remember the routines of their training — the inspections, the procedures, the social hierarchy of the hospital culture, the discipline, the rules and the penalties for getting caught breaking them. They might also concur that the function of the hospital training schools was actually twofold. Women were not only being trained for the nursing profession, but were also being inculcated with certain standards of decorum that had to do with respect, obedience and deference.

The young women in the photograph were indeed a cross between domestic servitude and devotional humility. As one historian of nursing describes it, hospitals were modeled on the middle-class household: 'Like daughters, or female servants, apprenticing students were expected to maintain the reputation of the family.'[2]

This photograph was taken between 1907 and 1910 on the lawn of the Provincial Hospital for the Insane in Toronto. The women were among the first students to attend the Training School for Nurses that had been newly instituted by the hospital's Medical Superintendent, Dr Charles Kirk Clarke. Dr Clarke had been appointed to his position in 1905.[3]

By 1907, the School was described as 'flourishing' and 'the nurses in training taking the keenest interest in the course.' Although the students would eventually be housed in their own separate residence, at the time of its founding, the student nurses lived on two hospital wards 'fitted up' for their occupancy.[4]

Staff training was not an entirely new concept at the Toronto Asylum. Dr Clarke's predecessor, Dr Daniel Clark, had encouraged it during his tenure as Medical Superintendent from 1875 to 1905. Clark had written a training manual entitled 'Handbook for

Dr. C.K. Clarke.

This portrait hangs in the stairwell of the Clarke Institute. The artist has cap-
tured Dr Clarke in an introspective moment Dr Clarke was very able with his
hands, and played as an amateur violinist with the Toronto Symphony
Orchestra, despite having lost two fingers of his right hand in a hunting accident when he was a teenager.[25]

Oil on canvas
Curtis A. Williamson, 1926

Attendants' in 1880 and later offered 'lectures on insanity' from 1892. These incentives, however, had been difficult to sustain owing to the low wages paid to the attendants and thus to frequent staff turnover. From 1893 to 1905, there had been only one 'trained infirmary nurse' at the Toronto Asylum.[5]

Dr C. K. Clarke, during his years as Medical Superintendent (1905-11), was determined to improve the quality of care for his patients. In the autumn of his first year, Clarke arranged for the appointment of a graduate nurse from a General Hospital, a Miss Marian Bethune, to oversee the creation of an in-house training facility for nurses at the Toronto Asylum. By 1906, 'a class had passed the primary examination...'[6] The photograph shown here is likely this first year class of nursing students.[7]

Dr Clarke, for whom the Clarke Institute for Psychiatry would later be named, was allegedly a progressive voice in mental health care at the time although his contribution to reform has been critically measured in recent times. He was also part of a larger movement of reforming physicians who were weary of political patronage and interference and intent upon improving the standards in their respective areas of expertise.[8]

Clarke was born in Elora, Ontario in 1857 and educated at the University of Toronto where he received his medical degree in 1879. As a young man he had worked with Dr Joseph Workman at the Provincial Asylum first as a Clinical Assistant and later as Assistant Physician. Clarke would maintain a lifelong affection for Dr Workman whom he later described as 'the greatest man I have ever known.'[9]

Between 1881 and 1905, Clarke had played a critical role in the transformation of the Rockwood Hospital for the Insane in Kingston. In 1887 he had founded a Training School for Asylum Nurses at Rockwood that a contemporary described as pioneering, '...the seventh among such schools instituted in [North] America.'

While hospital training schools for nurses had existed in

Canada since 1874, the Rockwood was the first to prepare nurses specifically for the care of the mentally ill. The graduates of the program had assumed positions throughout the continent and Clarke was highly regarded for his progressiveness. Subsequently, similar training schools were established at both the Brockville and London Asylums.[10]

Clarke had also been instrumental, while at the Rockwood, of changing the name from 'Asylum' to 'Hospital for the Insane.' He would later write, '...the basis of our teaching is the hospital idea — that is, the patients are regarded as sick people and are treated as such. Both patients and nurses are taught this.'[11] Clarke recognized that a change in name was essential for a change in perception and in the quality of care.

The provincial government, in 1907, adopted Clarke's recommendation for their other facilities throughout Ontario. The provincial 'Asylums' became 'Ontario Hospitals for the Insane' and the 'mental cases' became 'patients' and not 'inmates' of the Asylum system.[12]

Similarly by 1911, consistent with Clarke's 'hospital idea,' there were departmental training schools for nurses at all of the Ontario Hospitals. These programs included yearly provincial examinations and provision for the instruction of male attendants in the fundamentals of nursing care.[13] Patient care had been traditionally segregated by gender. In 1912 however, during the tenure of Dr. Clarke's successor, Dr. J. M. Forster, the women nursing graduates were being regularly assigned to the men's admission ward.[14]

The 'ideal nurse for mental cases', Clarke lectured in 1906, should possess 'kindness, tact, infinite patience, sympathy and truthfulness...' Before the Nurses' Alumnae Association of Toronto, Clarke described the ideal nurse in terms of her character. She was to be the embodiment of all the exemplary qualities of the nurturing woman. Clarke's 'hospital idea' did however

3. Temperature, Pulse & Recording
A nursing team at work, about
1910, in the Howard block. Notice
the patient chart and a landscape
picture on the wall. The picture is
probably a print, but chosen for a
gracious and soothing effect.

Glass negative (F)
Reproduced by permission
CAMH, AHCP&MHS

anticipate a more substantial role for the nurse in mental health care. Her skills and knowledge were understood to be as important as her ideal character traits.[15]

Her training was designed to be 'most thorough and complete' consisting of 'a careful course in general medicine, and in mental disease, by the hospital staff.' At the pioneering Rockwood School, which was the prototype for the later Training Schools, the nursing students took additional courses from Queen's University Medical Department. They were 'obliged to pass a careful examination, written and oral' before graduating from the program.[16]

Clarke wrote, 'The very best nurses for mental cases, or indeed for all classes of cases, were those who had passed a period of probation in the care of the insane and graduated in an up-to-date General Hospital.' The probationary period served to teach the nurse flexibility and 'the ability to lead and persuade,' what Clarke called 'psycho-therapeutics.' He had observed nurses who had not had the benefit of working with the mentally ill and found they '...did not seem to get in touch with their patients ...' and had '...no real knowledge of the true nature of insanity ...'[17] He had consulted with colleagues in other settings and found that his observations were essentially correct.

In his 1906 Report he wrote, 'If it were possible to have the General Hospitals in Ontario give graduates of our training schools opportunity to take a post graduate course and establish reciprocal relations between general hospital training schools and Hospital for Insane training schools, good results would follow.'[18] What had stood in the way of such innovations, in Clarke's view, was 'popular prejudice' creating 'stumbling blocks in the way of advanced treatment for the most helpless class in the community.' Clarke was describing what we would now call the 'stigma of mental illness' that continues to be an obstacle to enlightened mental health care to this day. Clarke wrote, 'In training our nurses there is one thing never lost sight of for a moment, and from the beginning to the end of the term, the truth that all forms of insanity must be regarded as disease, as well marked as typhoid, is impressed upon them.' This was the essential tenet of Clarke's 'hospital idea' for the treatment of mental illness.

The nursing care consisted of a variety of therapeutic measures. Ideally, the patient should enjoy 'isolation' understood as a separation from 'the importunities of anxious, injudicious friends.' Privacy, quiet, rest, careful feeding and massage were all part of the therapy. The hospital was to be like an attentive household.

Clarke maintained that if the physical needs of his patients were addressed, then mental problems could be lessened or alle-

4. Men's Ward, about 1910.

The person sitting at the table is probably the matron of the hospital — she is wearing the uniform dress but not an apron, thus indicating that she is engaged primarily in administrative work. The Queen Street Infirmary for men was completed in 1893. Glass negative (D), reproduced by permission CAMH, AHCP&MHS

viated. Thus body weight, nutrition, fluid balance and bowel movements were carefully monitored and recorded. Above all, the nurse from his training school was taught that each patient in her care was a 'special study' requiring flexibility and honesty. She was part of a new paradigm in 'advanced treatment.'[19]

It is of particular interest to the history of the nursing profession in Ontario, that Ontario Hospital Training Schools were a result of medical initiative. The general hospital schools had been differently conceived. These latter facilities were largely inspired and influenced by the ideas of Florence Nightingale. Nightingale had organized the first program for training nurses in Great Britain in mid-nineteenth century. Her *Notes on Nursing*, originally published in 1859, was seminal in the formation of a nurse-led profession and was hugely influential on both sides of the Atlantic.[20]

The Graduate Nurses' Association of Ontario, as early as 1905, had been concerned about the physical well being of the mentally-ill patient and included 'Asylum care as appropriate work for its members.' But it would not be until 1922, that the Ontario Nurses' Registration Act was passed that 'provided guidance for training schools for nurses and laid the groundwork for standardization of nurses' education.'

With this legislation, 'all graduate nurses [in Ontario] from approved schools of nursing, whether located in psychiatric hospitals or general hospitals, were eligible to work in either kind of setting.'[21] The Training School for Nurses at the Ontario Hospital in Toronto would continue to train students for the nursing profession until 1936.

The young women in the photograph were part of a new model in the care of the mentally ill for the period. They were also entering the workforce at a time when middle-class and unmarried women generally stayed within the home and family. The new professional identity, symbolized by the uniforms and the

5. Women's Ward, about 1910.

The Queen Street Infirmary for women, completed 1895. The beds are about 6 inches closer together on this ward. Structural iron pillars showing between windows.

regimented apprenticeship program, was being fostered against certain social realities.

Kathryn McPherson writes, 'Together, the uniform, the rules, the disciplinary measures and the celebration of 'character' helped nursing administrators mould apprentices into a labour force that was expandable, skilled, inexpensive, subordinate and respectable.'[23]

From within their collective identity, these young women were part of an emerging culture. Unwittingly perhaps, they were on the cusp of two historical narratives. The first refers to the modern hospital, particularly the 'hospital for the insane,' as a legitimate place for the diagnosis, treatment and care of the mentally ill. The second, the ascent of the professionally trained nurse to replace unskilled attendants, served this legitimizing process.

Further, by utilizing professional nurses, the hospital was providing for a category of employment uniquely adaptable to the needs of women. Nursing provided an adequate salary in a non-industrial setting. It commanded public respect, the chance to travel and, 'in the modern economy, the option of leaving and rejoining the paid work-force without substantial penalty.'[24]

In shifting so profoundly from the moral economy of the family to the political economy of the workplace, these young women found themselves, often unchaperoned, in the company of male physicians, attendants and patients. Further, the nature of the work was frequently of an intimate nature and offered to strangers.

The young women in the photographs needed to summon all their exemplary qualities of character and their new professional prestige to survive in these perilous waters. The expression on their faces speaks volumes and makes of the pictures an invaluable document in the history of nursing.

. TEN .

FROM 999 TO 1001 QUEEN STREET: A CONSISTENTLY VITAL RESOURCE

PREVIOUS CHAPTERS HAVE CHRONICLED the early years at what is now known as the Queen Street site of the Centre for Addiction and Mental Health. Physical upgrades for Queen Street's diversified therapeutic mission — still in progress as we celebrate the sesqui-centenary — were a long time in coming. A 1937 study commissioned from U.S. experts reported that the Ontario Hospital (OH) network on the whole had sunk 'to a lamentable plane of incapacity.' At the Ontario Hospital, Toronto (OHT) as it was known from 1919 to 1966, they observed overcrowding as elsewhere, and little change in physical plant from the nineteenth century or the end of Dr. Daniel Clark's era. The stigma surrounding mental illness and associated therapeutic modalities had long existed. As noted by the 1937 study: 'The unpleasant feeling that many citizens have about this old hospital can hardly be dissipated.'[1]

This suggested that it was necessary for the government to shift its thinking rather than proceed with incremental improvements to the building stock. Indeed Dr. C. K. Clarke had urged, from 1906, that the OHT should relocate elsewhere and sell the site 'to a railroad or other purchaser'. Queen Street was far from unique. Lakeshore was 'so crowded that it functions poorly' while the Toronto Psychiatric Hospital (TPH — forerunner of the Clarke Institute) was 'too small for its purpose and not well arranged.' Also criticizing the system's centralized political and bureaucratic structure, the authors anticipated by half a century the future of a lay community advisory board that would be fol-

1. Aerial View, before 1954.

This view from the north west shows the central complex of nineteenth century structures, interior roads and landscaping. Not shown are the perimeter walls, lodges and farm outbuildings. The latter were located just below the centre-foreground where rectangular garden plots are visible.

Reproduced by permission CAMH, AHCP&MHS

lowed by an independent governing board.[1]

The Second World War was followed by peacetime economic and social resurgences. At mid-century, Queen Street marked its first 100 years of service. Yet in 1950 a special committee similar to a Royal Commission noted problems throughout the province-wide fleet of 14 Ontario Hospitals plus TPH that left 'no room for complacency.' The OHT was among those most over-crowded, with an in-patient population of 1,167 (men and women almost equally) that exceeded its rated bed capacity by 56%. While approving of the grounds and not commenting on the architecture, the committee did feel that a great deal of remedial work was clearly needed inside. 'While each Ontario mental hospital is pleasantly situated in parklike grounds, the interiors of most buildings tend to be drab and depressing.'[2] Six years later at OHT, however, the interiors of the 'Old Hospital Building and Cottages' remained problematic. The Inspector reported that their interior state was 'rather deplorable' and greatly in need of 'a complete renovation,' which was due to a lack of remedial maintenance, rather an any reflection on the housekeeping staff.[3]

Committee on New Construction for Hospitals

The government of Leslie Frost and his Ministries of Health and of Public Works had set about responding on a number of fronts. Professor Eric Arthur was appointed to chair a committee that published guidelines in 1954 on new construction for general and specialty hospitals. Regrettably they were not mandated to address refurbishing of existing facilities or their adaptive re-use.[4] At OHT the Province built the Reception Wing (a.k.a. Administration Building) in 1954-56 to the design of Mathers & Haldenby. Vitally needed in-patient, therapeutic and clinical support components were welcomed into a functional if stylistically rather plain structure. Three storeys high and 600 feet long, it ran parallel to the Howard building, completely dominating the frontage along Queen Street.

That decision by Public Works on the location of the Administration Building, although not remarked upon at the time, might be said in retrospect to have signalled the demise of the Howard and Tully structures. A design regime showing greater respect for the 19th century's built legacy would instead

2. Aerial View, after the Administration Building was opened in 1956.
A view from a similar position to the earlier aerial photograph. The Administration
Building is now fronting the site along Queen Street, and surrounded by a signifi-
cant increase in paved parking with a concomitant loss of trees and landscaping.
Reproduced by permission CAMH, AHCP&MHS

have located the Administration Building along one or more of the
open expanses just inside the east, south and west walls. The
overall effect was akin to placing a new office building on Front
Street and hiding Toronto's Beaux Arts masterpiece Union
Station. At Queen Street, all of Howard's original front elevation
was now obscured except for the landmark dome and Ward 8
directly below it. Lawns and gardens formerly fronting the

Howard building were paved over for parking lots. A multi-level covered walkway linking to the Reception Wing was punched into the north elevation of Howard's building.[5] The implication was clear and unmistakable.

Attitudes and the OHT building legacy

How and why had the official attitudes become so cavalier toward Queen Street's distinctive architectural legacy? Let us consider four broad, inter-related patterns that may have been factors

Firstly, after the Second War many aspects of life were strongly influenced by a firm belief in modernity for its own sake. The new, it was held, could almost single-handedly achieve social improvements and offer relief from oppressive environments.

Secondly, commencing in 1951, there was a dramatic change in the clinical technology for treating and managing mental illness through the widespread introduction of tranquilizing drugs (psychotropics or neuroleptics).[6] In addition to bringing great improvements in the prognosis for schizophrenia and other psychoses (representing a significant majority of OH clients), this advancement allowed a shift away from the earlier emphases on the confinement of patients for extended lengths of time and the need for strong physical security within institutions. Fundamentally as well, this technology was less radical in application than the preceding decades of experimentation with interventions like insulin coma, metrazol convulsion therapy, 'prolonged narcosis, electroplexy [and] psychosurgery'.[7] The benefits of the newer pharmaceuticals encouraged public general hospitals to overcome their resistance to establishing community psychiatric units,[8] spurred on by Federal and Provincial policy changes and special grant funding. This began the very next year, 1952.

An important consequence was a substantial reduction

3. Aerial View from the north-east, 1971.

Construction has started on two of the Treatment units, and on the Community Centre within the old quadrangle. The Superintendent's residence can still be seen in the foreground, lower left of photograph.

between 1952 and 1972 in the unrelenting, century-old pressure to increase admissions and maintain large long-stay populations — forces that constantly combined to exceed the built capacities of provincial psychiatric hospitals (PPHs). By the close of that two-decade period at Queen Street the actual resident population had declined from a high of 1,200 in the 1950s to the early-1973 level of 440 inpatients.[9]

Thirdly, clinical professionals and administrators were determined to combat the stigma long associated with mental illness and its institutions. They wanted to improve patient living conditions, public attitudes and support in the community. They also wanted staff professional prestige to be enhanced to a degree more in line with their counterparts practising in physical medicine and general hospitals.

And finally, there was a change in ideas about what constituted appropriate architecture and design for mental hospitals. Dr. Burdett McNeel, the province's chief mental health official from 1957 to 1966, was keenly interested in the field's long history. In 1960 he posited that there had been four distinct eras of mental hospital construction in Ontario, each of them characterized by 'radical architectural changes': first in the latter half of the 19th century, large buildings were the norm; then came 'small communities of detached cottages', citing Whitby (1913-20) as an example; thirdly, those built 'just before and after the Second World War [which] are sprawling establishments characterized by large areas of glass, tile, terrazzo, stainless steel, and by long corridors.' As to the fourth model: 'A new architectural phase is now beginning, with the designing of smaller regional hospitals.'[10]

The key significance here for this categorization lies in how Ontario's chief psychiatric official regarded the structures at Queen Street. Clearly he saw them in terms of the first and third eras, and hence by then 'radically' out of date. Moreover this was a view that McNeel imparted to his Minister from 1958 to 1968,

Dr. Matthew Dymond, as well as to his colleagues and many others. In a 1960 article Dr. Bill Henderson agreed that the stigma of mental illness remained strong, along with a stigma on the mental hospital itself which, with its 'threat of isolation ... has added impetus to the development of other facilities in the community,' particularly a burgeoning of psychiatric units in general hospitals.[11]

Development of forward plans in the 1960s

By 1961, O.H. Toronto remained one of the three PPHs that still remained overcrowded.[12] In his 1959 'blueprint' master plan for mental health services, Minister Dymond had set a moratorium on new beds at 'the existing large hospitals' while launching a joint Architecture Committee of Health and Public Works staff to develop proposals for the design of new and expanded hospital facilities.[13] In the meantime the perception of OHT as 'massive' was addressed in part through an operational rather than physical decentralization. The patient treatment units were divided into geographic catchment areas that shared centralized support services, labs, therapeutic facilities and administration. These shared services were primarily situated in the Administration Building and two small, 20th century outbuildings, while the patients' residential and treatment units were largely confined to the 19th century historic structures. And the latter remained, as observed in 1950, 'drab and depressing.' In the 1960s they were still overcrowded and, even if that were corrected, were considered too large for a modern psychiatric hospital which should have an optimum of 250 to 300 beds.[14]

When was the actual decision made to proceed with demolition? Burdett McNeel, anticipating the 1961 Progressive Conservative Convention, reported on mental health achievements under Dymond's Ministry, in one case to a Progressive Conservative Party official. While his memo of October, 1960 made no mention of major work at Queen Street, his letter to the Conservative Party official in October, 1961 did note that: 'A proposal to break up the large mental hospital into units that are essentially semi-autonomous small hospitals has been implemented at the Ontario Hospitals at New Toronto, Hamilton and Toronto.' Then the following month he wrote again to Dymond attaching a report of construction work and planning during the Minister's term of office that chronicled plans being drawn for a number of facilities, the future Clarke Institute among them, and also including: 'Re-building of Ontario Hospital, Toronto.'[15]

While Dr. Paul Christie settled in as Superintendent the following year, McNeel pronounced on the timing of these projects. Construction was to commence in 1963 for the Ontario Psychiatric [Clarke] Institute and 'reconstruction' of the OHs at London (600 beds) and Toronto (900 beds). Any ambiguity around the meaning of 're-building' and 'reconstruction' was soon dispelled. Christie and McNeel met in the latter's office during August, 1962 with the Public Works architectural staff concerning the Queen Street Project, 'to further discuss . . . the demolition of the old buildings block and the requirements for rebuilding.'[16]

Those dramatic plans were announced publicly in 1964. The Department of Health's Annual Report for that and subsequent years made clear that 'planning is continuing for the replacement of certain obsolete accommodation, e.g. the Ontario Hospital, Toronto, and parts of the Ontario Hospital, Penetanguishene.' The 1966 Annual Report left no doubt that the whole of the facility (not part, as at Penetanguishene) was at stake: 'Preliminary plans for the reconstruction of the Ontario Hospital, Toronto, have been prepared and submitted.'[17]

Implementation of Building Plans

The actual work was slow to materialize. Plans for Queen Street assumed a lower priority than construction of the TPH's replacement facility, the Clarke Institute, and for the under-serviced areas surrounding Goderich, Owen Sound and South Porcupine where new PPHs sprang up. In 1965 Dr. Dymond commissioned from a consultant, Dr. Ian Urquhart, 'a searching study' into the OH system and the Ministry. Urquhart was scathing in his general assessment of 'original hospital buildings' that were 'still standing and in use'. At best they provided 'almost passable accommodation, in spite of the difficulties inherent in the original solid construction.' Moreover the worst of 'these old buildings have had little done to them and indeed little can or should be done ...These buildings should be destroyed, and proper accommodation with adequate rehabilitative facilities be developed as soon as possible.'[18]

Dr. Henderson, McNeel's successor from 1966 as head of Mental Health services, supported the thrust of those recommendations. In his paper read to the Canadian Psychiatric Association's annual meeting in 1967, Henderson reminded his colleagues that: 'The institution known . . . more popularly by the address, 999 Queen Street, is now scheduled for demolition, to be replaced by a psychiatric centre which will embody the most modern and advanced concept of design and treatment for the mentally ill.'[19]

Public attitudes towards mental illness remained an important issue. A *Toronto Life* article in 1968 typified the era's media coverage and public perceptions. It was illustrated (as seldom permitted now) by five photos of patients whose glum, impoverished appearance contrasted starkly with the toney, up-market crowd featured elsewhere in the magazine. The article's text evoked a century of myths. One patient was quoted on that theme: 'I used to drive by this place and think, "You'll never find me in that goddamn nuthouse." But this is my third trip around here now. I'm an alcoholic, y'see.. I only wish it was a different address like 1239 Queen, or something. That 999 is like a goddamn tattoo.'[20]

Such thinking was commonplace.

In 1967 the architectural firm of Somerville, McMurrich & Oxley had undertaken a master plan in consultation with Dr. Christie and his staff, along with the Mental Health Division and architects in the public works ministry. The physical design was informed by the renowned work, notably at the Saskatchewan Psychiatric Centre in Yorkton, of Dr. Humphry Osmond and architect Kyo Izumi.[21] Architect Loren Oxley described the role of the complex's centrepiece:

> The Community Centre will become an important element in the overall treatment program. Along with the recreational and therapeutic facilities that it contains (swimming pool, gymnasium, etc.) it will also feature a bank, beauty parlour, sidewalk cafe and other services — all in an enclosed 'shopping mall' type of setting. All of those facilities will be for use by the patients. Because it will so closely approximate the 'world outside', and because of the regular contact with outside local residents using the facilities, the patients will be introduced back into the complexities of social relationships in a controlled environment.[22]

4. Construction of the Community Centre, 1971.
The Tully West Wing can be seen, photograph taken from a vantage point on the East wing.

Photograph by *realization*, Toronto
Reproduced by permission CAMH, AHCP&MHS

Assessment of the Environment, 1970s

An independent, university-based study was launched in 1972 to record the socio-cultural impacts of Queen Street's built environment on a comparative basis between the old and, as it steadily emerged, the new. Employing the neutral, non-intrusive methodology of participant-observation pioneered by Erving Goffman,[23] Dr. Kelner and her associates (this writer among them) found that patients and staff who had experienced both settings held 'strong reactions against' the old facility, 'particularly when they compared it with the new one'. Their comments centered around its atmosphere of hopelessness, its resemblance to a jail and its 'depressing effects on their feelings.'[24]

5. Patient's Room in Active Treatment Unit(ATU) Two, 1973. A chaplaincy student relaxes on the window seat while visiting a patient's room with another staff member, shortly after the building opened. J.G. Howard's 1850 building and its dome, demolished in 1976, are visible through the window.
Reproduced by permission CAMH, AHCP&MHS

6. Treatment Unit One and West Tully Wing, 1972.
Photograph shows the Treatment Unit when first occupied, before the Tully
or Howard buildings were demolished. Excavations for Treatment Units
Three and Four will begin shortly and will require demolition of the Tully
wings.

Photographer: Roy Nicholls
Reproduced by permission CAMH, AHCP&MHS

The results after the initial, 1970-72 phase of demolition,
construction and moving into the first of the new treatment units
and the community centre were immediate and dramatic. Queen
Street's first-ever attempt at hospital accreditation, despite coming in the midst of the initial phase of the move in 1972, was successful. New staff recruitment and extended lengths of employment were directly linked to the combined effects of the new
facilities and general revitalization as 'an important factor in
attracting new people of the top rank.' One staff member
remarked: 'Professionals are starting to see us as a place to refer
people, not just as a dumping ground.'[25] In general, 'the move
into the new buildings, combined with the new treatment pro-

grammes, has generated considerable enthusiasm, pride and hope among the staff.'[26]

The Tully Wings and several other 19th century structures were demolished starting in 1970. The Ontario Heritage Foundation in 1975 put forward a proposal from architect Jack Diamond with detailed plans for adaptively reusing the surviving 1850 Howard building.[27] Diamond argued for changing the usage of the old structure, returning it in part to the tasks that Howard had intended. The proposal also argued for the demolition of the 1956 Administration Building.

Despite its merits and heated debate, this proposal was opposed by the government and did not succeed. Politically the timing was wrong; commitments had been made that could not be revoked. Implementation of plans for the 'complete replacement' of historic fabric by modern buildings went forward.[28]

7. Staff meeting in a Treatment Unit.
Staff felt renewed enthusiasm for their work in the new buildings.

Reproduced by permission CAMH, AHCP&MHS

The Future of the Queen Street Site

Studies over the past twenty years have been consistent on two points. Firstly, there was agreement that Queen Street continued to fulfill a vital psychiatric facility need — one that was quite distinctive, even from other hospitals having a defined role in psychiatric care. For example, in 1996 the Toronto District Health Council (DHC) reported the following utilization data for 1993/94 in respect of all facilities that provided psychiatric inpatient treatment (i.e., not including the range of Queen Street's and other outpatient and community-based services).

UTILIZATION COMPARISONS AMONG INSTITUTIONS, 1994

Psychiatric Inpatient Indicators	Queen Street Mental Health Centre	Clarke Institute	Total for 20 Metro Toronto General Hospitals
No. of Approved Beds	477	80	677
Total Year Number of Inpatient Days of Stay	186,766	29,189	222,349
Average Days of Stay	129.4	32.4	16.8

This table makes clear that Queen Street remained unique in providing a high proportion of the region's overall psychiatric inpatient care. Moreover its clients were more severely ill than those of the Clarke and the 20 general hospital wards.

The second consistent issue was a persistent belief in what the Centre's next developmental stage should be: a divestment from provincial control to governance by a voluntary board. As Simmons observed at the end of the 1980s, however: 'One of the most puzzling aspects of mental health policy is that while there has been near-unanimous support for divestment of the provincial psychiatric hospitals, government has been reluctant to act.'[29] Several years later the Toronto DHC's recommendations for hospital restructuring and mental health planning proved decisive, as supported by the province's Health Services Restructuring Commission (HSRC). In a clear vote of confidence in the Centre, the DHC recommended realigning the catchment areas with Whitby PPH to give Queen Street responsibility for all of Metro Toronto. In addition, 'the province should divest itself of Queen Street Mental Health Centre and establish it as a community hospital which continues providing the services normally assigned to provincial psychiatric hospitals.'[30]

Queen Street had previously undergone one amalgamation through absorbing the catchment area and several active programs of Lakeshore PPH, closed by the government in 1979.[31] The HSRC took matters to the next stage in 1997 through mandating Queen Street's amalgamation the following year with its allied psychiatric facility, the Clarke Institute, and the province's two leading addiction institutions, the Addiction Research Foundation and the Donwood Institute. Despite the trauma of significant downsizing, the new Centre for Addiction and Mental Health (CAMH) has determined that the merger was successful. In 1999, CAMH was designated by the World Health Organization as a Centre of Excellence in Addictions and Mental Health, one of only four in the world, and was awarded a maximum, three-year accreditation.[32] Soon after, the CAMH Board of Directors announced its intention 'to seriously assess redeveloping the Centre using the Queen Street site as a 'hub' for Centre operations.'[33] The institution's future will then link in unbroken continuity with the first patients who arrived on 26 January 1850.

. ELEVEN .

ASYLUM LAYOUTS

by Edna Hudson

THE PROPER STUDY OF ARCHITECTURE is concerned with much more than merely historic, aesthetic and stylistic matters. When analyzing for example, broad changes in the design of places to house and treat those with mental illness — formerly called asylums — the findings can illuminate shifts in practices of patient management, and in staff patient relations. They also track the adaptability of that architecture to a vast array of changing circumstances.

Architecture, as a discipline, is not usually taught as such an intensive study of the relationships between function and built form. A modern approach of that type is sorely needed and a start has been made, notably by Bill Hillier.[1] Hillier's approach is a direct study of buildings in light of relevant social theories that inform us as to their desired utility and function. Appreciative of his work, I will formulate some statements on how structures built expressly for those with mental illness have affected the lives of those who live and work in them.

While theories are the means by which new applications usually arise in science, this is not so in architecture. For architecture has a rather high artistic and social content. And while it cannot be practised as a science, the output — realized buildings, can be subjected to theoretical analyzes.

Spatial configuration of structures is important for two reasons. It influences patterns of movement, and, it identifies who will be available for social interaction — referred to as co-presence. Patterns of movement come about, as the result of the placement of doors and walls. Patterns of co-presence and co-awareness are particular to a spatial design, and alter with building function. Co-present people may not know each other, may not acknowledge each other, but their coexistence is a fact and a resource. The analysis of that spatial configuration is the most promising path from architecture for it can shed much light on the building's social effects.

For example, consider the effect of a corridor's length in hospitals. In a building designed with short corridors, the sight lines down the corridor will be short. So, most encounters will take place relatively suddenly, with little time to asses the pending encounter. Long corridors, with correspondingly long sightlines will give rise to different encounters, often more comfortable ones. This is due to the time available to evaluate the situation and compose a response. So behavioural differences can be induced and so alter the plan — by configurational change. What is normal behaviour in one spatial configuration may not be in another. It can also be surmised that the human mind makes inferences

1. Views of Hospitals visited by Howard
(above) State Lunatic Hospital, Worcester, Mass. Opened 1833
(below) Utica State Lunatic Asylum, New York. Opened 1843

from spatial configuration. Long sight lines are instinctively safer because one knows that one can not be so readily surprised.

Moral Therapy and architecture

The ideal layout for any responsible treatment, should promote the well-being of patients, and even their cure. In 1848 John Connolly[2] recommended that every patient should be treated kindly, that there should be good surveillance at all times, and that patients should be classified by symptom and should be sheltered from the injurious spectacle of any other patient class. Patients were not to be physically restrained but allowed to mix socially with others of their (diagnostic) class and gender, in a soothing and attractively dignified environment. The restoration of a patient to health was assumed to flow from the ideal environment and interaction with Nature. Health did not flow from introspective analysis nor the formation of strong human bonds with other patients nor the use of heroic purgative, drug treatments nor physical interference. Patients classified as Curable, or Recovering, were allowed more time with staff, physician and matron, and given meaningful work within the asylum. The assumption was that kindness itself was curative.

The typical architectural response needed to allow the Connolly program to be effective, was a building that emphasized its pastoral setting, and had available: multiple segregated stairs; wide corridors for leisurely walks, socializing and the consolations of religion. In light of this, let us consider the plan of Howard's building with reference to the plans of others institutions that he had collected prior to laying-out of his asylum. These are Hanwell Asylum, Middlesex, England; Island Retreat or Pauper Lunatic Asylum, Blackwell Island, New York; Utica State Hospital, New York; Howard is also known to have visited Worcester State Hospital, Massachusetts; and Pennysylvania Hospital, Philadelphia.

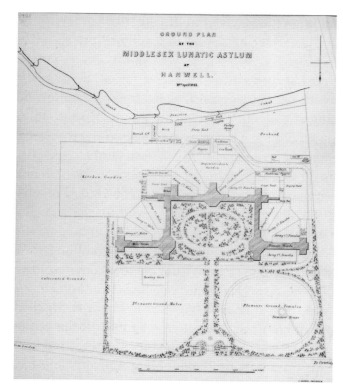

2. Ground Plans
(left) Middlesex
Lunatic Asylum
at Hanwell, Mx,
England,
(below)
Pennysylvania
Hospital for the
Insane at
Philadelphia.

Toronto
Reference
Library, Howard
Collection
(left) 459.21
(below) 459.32

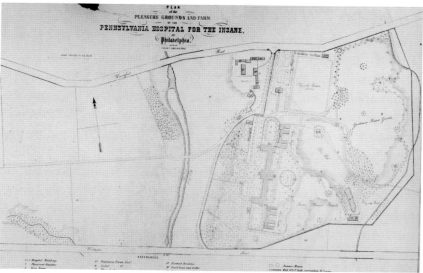

The Spatial Reality at the Asylum in Toronto.

The land having been acquired in 1844, the first problem that engages the architect is where to locate the building on the site. This low-lying 50 acres was formerly the grounds of the Garrison Military Reserve, and extended south from Queen Street toward the lake. The land was not distinguished by prominent features such as any dramatic changes in elevation, standing water nor major stream. The siting was determined by a host of factors. The institution had to be self-sufficient as to water supply so being approximate to the lake was crucial. Further, Howard was reassured that the complex would indeed be growing so that the first phase must be a building as close to Queen Street as could be tolerated so that its location did not impinge on later building.[3] But that concern was tempered by the fact that the central administration building had to be sufficiently visible to be understood in the public mind. As well, in part it had to shelter the patients whether at leisure or in other activities, from the prying eyes of the general public. The location had as well to be convenient for the suppliers, tradesmen and visitors. So, the building was to be close to Queen Street but removed from it. Howard's compromise — a 300 foot set-back from the Queen Street road allowance.

Next, the orientation of the building would be considered. Howard chooses to build on an axis parallel to the lake. This affords inhabitants the best views over the lake, enhancing the contemplation of the changing glories of Nature. This overall orientation involves a long south facing elevation, and perhaps some over-exposure to the sun. Howard decently moderates this by projecting sections of the structure forward providing some shade.

A U-shaped building is decided upon, to house three to four hundred patients. The U configuration allows good outward-looking views. Most of the other designers in Howard's collection of plans for other asylums employ it. Hanwell is the only one that places the main entrance on the concave side of the U, while at Toronto and Worcester, the main entrance is on the convex side.

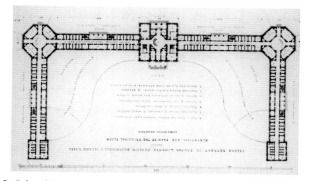

3. Island Retreat Pauper Lunatic Asylum, New York. Plan.

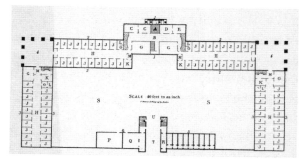

4. State Lunatic Asylum, Worcester,
Massachussets. Plan.

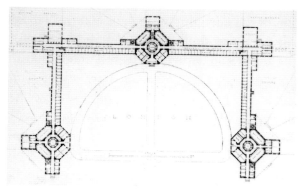

5. Middlesex Lunatic Asylum, Hanwell, England. Plan.

The outside world is much less visible and of less concern to patients in Howard's scheme.

A corridor runs the length of the Howard building, and provides an exercise path for patients. At 14 feet wide it is wider than any of the US hospitals Howard visited in 1844, except possibly Worcester (**fig. 4**). The rest have corridor widths of eight and ten feet. The plans of the Hanwell Asylum show clearly that corridors there are ten feet wide. The greater width would encourage perambulation by a good number of patients, and perhaps increase the number of chance encounters or patterns of co-presence. John Connolly recommended setting out a few tables and chairs in the corridor. But the habit of crowding it with a static tableau of furniture is evidence of sad overpopulation of the institution. Surely it is also a counter-productive move, away from Moral Therapy

At Hanwell (**fig. 5**) the gallery(read corridor) is single loaded, so that it has a wall lined with windows, offering therapeutic views to the ambulatory of the surrounding countryside. In Howard's design, the corridor is partially single-loaded. There are dining rooms and day rooms on the south side of the building to be sure, but punctuated with corridor windows that give an excellent view of the lake. It is remarkable that none of the US asylums visited by Howard on his 1844 tour have exterior windows in the corridor, they are all built on the claustrophobic, parsimony-driven model of a double loaded corridor. At Hanwell, the galleries in the wings are on the outside of the U, thus affording good views, while in Toronto the galleries designed for wings look across to the opposite wing. This may have been decided because the airing courts for patients were on the other side of the building. Regular pastoral activities such as drawing water from wells and herding farm animals can be seen from corridor windows.

An outstanding and very beautiful feature of the Toronto Asylum was a large semi-circular verandah at each end of the building. This feature was also to be found in the Worcester State

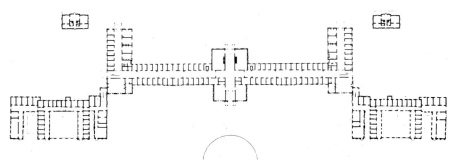

6. Plan of Principal Story, Pennsylvania Hospital for the Insane.
Toronto Reference Library, Howard Collection 459.33

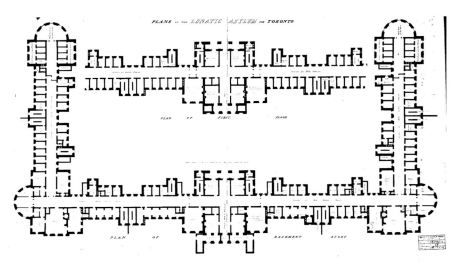

7. Plans of the Lunatic Asylum in Toronto.
Drawings signed by John Howard, 1845.
Archives of Ontario 4699, RG 15-13-2-40

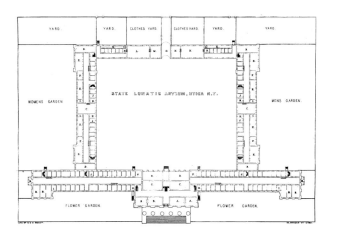

8. Plan of State
Lunatic Asylum,
Utica, N.Y.
Toronto Reference
Library, Howard
Collection 459.41

Asylum (**fig. 4**) which Howard visited, so it had been climate test-
ed, and found suitable.

All the institutions studied had indoor plumbing — water-
closets, washrooms and bath rooms although too few in number
by modern standards. The closets(toilets) were connected to sewers, and in Howard's building each was fitted with what was
referred to as Roe's patent mechanism. At the time strong odours
were always associated with these closets, due to less than fastid-
ious users and infrequent manual flush. Howard's drawings show
he planned to have the watercloset projecting out from the footprint of the building perhaps to increase air circulation.
Unfortunately they were built fully contained within the structure.
There was both hot and cold running water at the Toronto Asylum
from the time the building opened, available from a storage tank
holding 12,000 gallons in the dome. Water was pumped up to both
the Asylum and the New Garrison from a boiler, steam engine and
pump located at the foot of Strachan Avenue. Sufficient pressure
was generated by the reciprocating pump to raise the water 90
feet, to the top of the storage tank. The apparatus was run daily.
However the water may only have been available for restricted
hours, due to conservative ideas about what was appropriate. [4]

Within the Howard building were facilities for religious wor-
ship, as was the rule with all the institutions built at this time.
There were special benches at the back of each chapel for attendants, who sat ready to remove anyone causing a disturbance during a service. John Connolly[5] recommended that no asylum be
more than two stories, but given the budget and the numbers that
Howard was charged to house, he knew he had to break that
threshold. He took enormous care, by designing discrete systems
of staircases that separately connected from each floor to the
ground, that each floor could accommodate a different class of
patient. These exclusive staircases by-passed all the other floors
above and below. This feature perhaps uses space extravagantly,

but it is designed to contain each 'class' of patient within his or her own environment.

The current Toronto Asylum buildings.

The Administration building was built in 1956, has a library and offices on the ground floor and an auditorium was added to the front in 1980. The main administrative offices on the second floor have movable interior walls, which are a useful feature that supports administrative change. Individual rooms for sixty patients are on the top floor, each equipped with its own washroom. The building is in a bland modern style, of rose coloured brick and concrete. It cannot be described as any more than adequate. Yet it carries some architectural surprise in the mixture of functions that it was built to serve, and hence its layout.

The Community Centre was built in 1974, directly behind the Howard building. It comprises two gymnasiums and a swimming pool; an activity area and snack bar run by and for patients; a library for patients; and, a large staff cafeteria with a gallery above approached from inside the cafeteria.

The four new Treatment Units, built at the same time as the Community Centre are each distinct structures scattered throughout the grounds connected only at grade by walkways. Each is five stories, and capable of housing up to 175 patients. They are self-contained, each with its own classrooms, dining rooms, activity centres, treatment centres and offices for staff as well. Most of the patients on site are housed in these units

Space configuration and its effect on Asylum administration
Strong versus weak program.

There is no question but that both Howard's building and the Treatment Units were built to enforce a strong program of control. They were designed to support the aims of the staff.

Howard's building supported the premise that it was the task

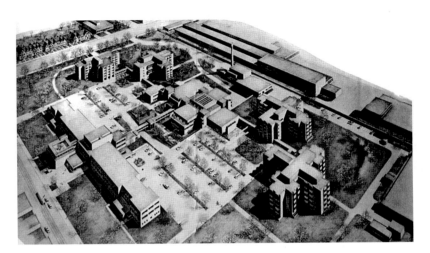

9. Architects' model of plans for Queen St. site.
Somerville, McMurrich & Oxley (1972)
The new construction was completed as shown here in concept. Not part of
the model, but surviving in fact are parts of the perimeter wall and two 19th
century storage buildings against the South wall. Nothing else remains of the
historical buildings

Reproduced by permission CAMH, AHCP&MHS

of the staff to control the patients by providing an environment
where the chief cause of excitement might be a change in the
weather. Each entrance to the building was associated with a specific route and destination. Patients had to know which door to
use to enter to get where they needed to go, not just any one would
do. Patients were not given much chance to feel in control of their
environment, they had no territory they could call their own.
Within the Treatment Units the staff have means to keep patients
under observation and control. These buildings have only one
door for entrance and exit, and the layout is designed to enhance
staff awareness of where the patients are at any time. The
Treatment Units have a repressive appearance. Every patient has
to complete a therapeutic program in a staff-determined length of
time.

The participants in a strong program will enjoy social strength within the institution and few segregated spaces will exist. The failure of such an environment is that the patients are institutionalized, incapable of making good life decisions for themselves. Institutions nearly always favour strong programs.

The Community Centre is as weakly programmed, as is the Administration Building. Both reinforce the premise that patients should have feelings of choice and control of their environment. Here anyone may interact with anyone else, a random pattern of meeting is normal. The general community is welcomed in, to share the amenities of the building with mental patients and staff, and increase the variety of co-presence that can be experienced. At the same time the staff presence is not controlling, and this has given rise to problems particularly in some of the recreational areas which tend to become segregated. The mentally ill are not co-equals of the wider community, they are easily preyed upon by those who seek an advantage, such as drug dealers. The solution lies in reintroducing staff presence into the trouble spots, or in better preparation of patients.

The Administration Building shows a weak program in many ways. None are denied entrance by the front door. Random interaction between staff and patients can occur at any time during business hours. The staff are mostly not involved in direct patient care, and so will not have strong ties to individual patients. Patients are not clearly marked off from other visitors to the building. The auditorium is used for a wide variety of events, from staff seminars, and patient concerts to film festivals.

Can a building be morphogenic?

The Administration Building was built directly in front of the Howard building — in places only 20 ft from it. The justification given for siting the new building there the was that the Howard building was intimidating, while a modern building was not. As regards Howard's facade, his portico — never built — would have given more grace to the front. The building was of white stone and brick, and if kept clean would have had a dignified presence. Several mature trees and a greenhouse were removed to make way for the new building.

In 1956, Howard's building still remained as the residential core of the Institution. The quality of these accommodations would have come under closer scrutiny, now that immediate comparisons could be made on a daily basis with the new ones in the Administration building. Patient rooms in the Treatment Units today do not have private bathrooms, neither did those in the Howard building. Highly visible and commented favourably upon by staff, the patient rooms in the Administration building do have private bathrooms. It was an unfortunate time for comparisons of this kind, for modernism was much admired in our culture at that time, as I have discussed elsewhere. [6]

For fifty years, little had been spent on maintenance of the Howard building. Nothing dreadful happened, it was a very sound structure though getting shabby. A factor in institutions is always that the inhabitants might not form positive attitudes towards their surroundings. There is some evidence that the patients were less than content with their housing in the old building. There is much more evidence that the staff became very hostile in their attitudes towards the old building.

The way in which patients are selected for an institution governs attitudes towards place, but not fear. Fear of place grows only from the way in which the building is used. Patients were more afraid of staff than of the building. Patients had little control over the way the building was used, staff had that control.

A fear among staff, unacknowledged, was that the institution itself would die, unless it was removed from the old buildings. This fear would has foundation the history of psychiatry, which from the earliest twentieth century has involved extraordinarily aggressive treatment protocols. The staff were afraid of the reminders that the building contained of therapies that were useless, of the often futile nature of their efforts to help the insane. A second factor was that for a long time, many of the staff had favoured moving the institution to another location, out of Toronto, on theories of therapeutic benefits of a cottage layout in pastoral surroundings. The institutional culture had thus for many years been pre-occupied with imagining a better reality awaiting them elsewhere. This culture looked for proof that they were right. They looked at the patients, who persisted in low rates of cure. And they saw also that the Howard building was not equal to their imaginings. So the reality for the staff was that the old buildings were frustrating their aspirations and desires.

It may seem odd that staff should be more aware of the possibility of death of the institution than patients, but the institution is created by staff. It continues daily to be re-created by them, in the normal expectation that they are creating an enduring monument, a monument that will outlive them. The institution itself shall be the fruit and proof of just and worthy endeavour. An institution that endures is also a powerful token of immortality.[7]

It is a popular belief that architecture can cause social unease, that an asylum or prison can bring about anti-social behaviour or induce stress and depression in individuals. Little is provable, and there is grounds for skepticism about any such link. In the 1972 - 73 Kelner experiment, a captive population of staff and patients was transferred from the old buildings to the (then) new Treatment Units. The methodology used no scales of measurement, and a discussion of the therapeutic experience of patients, or what might well be done differently in the same environment was not central to the inquiry. The vocabulary used to describe either building was not separated from the therapeutic hopes of patients. The theory of architectural determinism that underlay the study has never been substantiated experimentally.

Any building sets patterns of co-presence and co-awareness among its users, and sets some parameters of a virtual community. For safety there must be a presence of strangers (patients) as well as inhabitants (staff). An environment which separates inhabitants and strangers quite rigidly will generate environmental fear. To improve safety, there must be many opportunities for interface both within and between the groups. Environmental fear is the result of too few interface opportunities, and a weak virtual community.

If an institution such as Queen Street acquires a bad name, with social workers, police, neighbours etc., this will itself cut down interfacing within the institution. The social process of labeling and stigmatization is the prelude to a pathological community. 'To assign the socially weak and disadvantaged to places where visual signs of disorder are already present, will confirm the inferences people are already making from the signs of disorder.'[8] Obviously the patients suffer, but so also do the staff who choose to stay, and they are in a much stronger position to object to stigmatization, protest the 'signs of disorder', and bring about change.

The contrasts between the Howard building and the Administrative building were readily used in a process of stigmatization of the old building, gathering momentum with the realization that the institution must stay at its location on Queen Street. By 1975 the residential patients were housed in the new Treatment Units, and the Howard building stood empty. When the four Treatment Units took over the core function of the Howard building, the stage was set.

It was argued by the Ontario Heritage Foundation, abetted by the Toronto Historical Board, the Toronto City Council and a group of concerned citizens, that the Howard building should not be demolished, indeed that the Administration building should be demolished instead. Meetings took place between government representatives and all these groups, including the Architectural Conservancy of Ontario.[9] An architectural proposal was commissioned that supported the view that the Howard building might now be renovated and used as a weakly programmed, administration and activity building. The direct competition between the Howard and the Administration buildings was now apparent and took many by complete surprise. The old building was already publicly insulted and shamed by the propinquity of the newer building, its special qualities not understood and uncelebrated.

The renovation proposed by A. J. Diamond Associates was superb. It proposed some innovative changes to the spatial configuration, but the retention of many more, and a drastic change in function of the old building. It made 'use of almost all the old building's volumetric potentials.'[10]

Had that program been undertaken the Howard building would have reverted to uses similar to those intended by its creators. The historic building lost the contest for survival because most were unable to see that it could be so adapted.

EPILOGUE

THE INABILITY TO PRESERVE the fine 1846 structure at 999 Queen Street West stemmed from the difficulty of convincing public decision-makers that the bad image of a building was not a result of the building's structure. This proved to be an impossible task.

That there were problems retaining the building was obvious by October 1975. The Ontario Government had passed a new Heritage Act that year, yet government officials made it very clear that the Act would not be used to protect a provincially controlled building. A letter from the Government stated that 'the Heritage Act does not bind the Queen in Right of Ontario, and any new purported designation...is a nullity.'

The alternative to demolition and replacement was renovation as proposed by A. J. Diamond & Associates. However, the bad reputation of mental illness and failed health strategies to deal with it, overcame this cost-effective option.

It was not just the government of Bill Davis that was opposed to retaining this structure. Indeed Stephen Lewis and his colleagues in the New Democratic Party — the NDP was then the official Opposition in the Legislature — shared in this reluctance. When Frank Miller, the Minister of Health, announced on

December 17 that the government was not willing to delay demolition, Stephen Lewis remarked 'Right On.'

Premier William Davis interpreted protection of the old building as an attempt to deny good treatment to people who were mentally ill. His letter of 9 February 1976 stated:

> While the desire to designate and retain old edifices as part of our heritage is understandable, when two conflicting proposals arise, the prevailing response of the government must be to the needs of the people. In this instance the needs of the patients who are being treated now and those in the future are of paramount concern.

The conundrum which sealed the fate of 999 Queen lies at the heart of most struggles around heritage structures. Heritage is not always a popular issue and often it runs contrary to today's common wisdom, as well as its development pressures. The secret for 'living' heritage is obviously to try to find a balance between yesterday and tomorrow — the entirely human challenge which all of us face on a daily basis.

John Sewell,
18 September 2000.

CHAPTER 1 MADNESS & THE MEDIA 1840's —1890's
by Cyril Greenland

1. GEOFFREY Reaume *Remembrance of Patients Past* (Toronto: Oxford University Press, © 2000)

2. Dr. C.K. Clarke, for instance, denounced the 'employment of political hirelings'. Later, with reference to the proposed building of what became the Toronto Psychiatric Hospital, he wrote, 'it must be kept absolutely free from political control.' These quotations come from Cyril Greenland *Charles Kirk Clarke, A Pioneer of Canadian Psychiatry* (Toronto: The Clarke Institute of Psychiatry, 1966), p. 8

3. A brother of Daniel Hack Tuke (1827-1895) and great-grandson of William Tuke (1732-1819) founder of the York retreat in England. Quotation in C.G. Price 'A History of the Ontario Hospital, Toronto', M.S.W. Thesis, School of Social Work, University of Toronto, 1950; originally published in Daniel H.Tuke *The Insane in the United States and Canada* (London: 1885)

4. See Thomas E.Brown 'The origins of the Asylum in Upper Canada, 1830-1839.' *Canadian Bulletin of Medical History*, 1.1, pp. 27-56. Summer 1984.

5. Joseph Workman 'A Description of the Pestilent Conditions of the Toronto Lunatic Asylum in 1853' *The Sanitary Journal* II.1 p. 1-6 January 1876

6. C. Johnston *The Father of Canadian Psychiatry, Joseph Workman* (Victoria B.C.; Ogden press, © 2000)

7. For an account of the TGH Nervous or Psychopathic ward, founded by Dr D. Campbell Meyers, see R. Pos et al *Canadian Psychiatric Association J.* 20:5 1975.

8. C. Greenland 'Origins of the Toronto Psychiatric Hospital', in E.

Shorter, editor, *TPH: history and memories of the Toronto Psychiatric Hospital* (Toronto: Wall and Emerson, Inc, 1966), chapter 2

9.   Including Joan Sutton's piece, these quotations come from G. Baird '999 Queen Street: A Collective Failure of the Imagination*', City Magazine* 2 (3 and 4), 1976

10. Harvey G. Simmons *Unbalanced, Mental Health Policy in Ontario, 1930 - 1989* (Toronto: Wall and Thompson, © 1990)

11. I am grateful to Marg. Gorrie and the *Globe & Mail* for permission to reproduce extracts from her article.

CHAPTER 2   THE ASYLUM IN CONTEXT
William Hay's Architectural Overview (and Oversights) in *The Hand-Book of Toronto* in 1858[1]
by Douglas Scott Richardson

1.   A shorter version of this paper (titled 'The Politics of Architecture in 1858') was prepared for friends in 1986. In another form it was given as a lecture on four occasions in 1987: for the Continuing Education Department and the Archives of the Toronto Board of Education, in a symposium on 'Recent Research on Canadian Architecture' at the University of Toronto, to the annual conference of the Society for the Study of Architecture in Canada (again at U of T), and as the Napier B. Simpson, Jr., Memorial Lecture to the Architectural Conservancy of Toronto.

2.   The growth of Toronto's population, economy, and importance as regional centre has been studied, but not the enhancement of the image of the city in terms of its mid-century buildings. Factors cited for these boom years include development of the railways and the 'great fire' of 7 April 1849. The fire's immediate impact was limited to replacement of a few major buildings consumed between Church and George streets, from King to Adelaide (notably St James' Cathedral), and erection of new structures in place of others (chiefly St Lawrence Hall on the first city hall's

site). Another consequence was a comprehensive building by-law, following consultation with seven local architects. 'An Act to provide for the erection of Party Walls, and to prevent the Erection of Buildings dangerous in promoting Fires within certain limits' — neglected in Toronto literature — was passed by a city council newly aware of durable materials and sound construction on 25 January 1850. It is summed up (and misdated 28 January) in *Rowsell's City of Toronto and County of York Directory, for 1850-1...*, ed. J. Armstrong (Toronto: Henry Rowsell, 1850), pp. xxx-xxxii; see also John G. Howard's notice 'To Architects, Builders and Others', dated 21 May 1850, in ibid., p. 170 (both references courtesy of Shirley Morriss); *The Journal of John George Howard, 1833-49*, ed Shirley G. Morriss, 7 vols. in 3 ([Toronto: Ontario Heritage Foundation], n.d. [1987]), vol. 7, p. 31, n. 7; and Frederick H. Armstrong, *A City in the Making: Progress, People & Perils in Victorian Toronto* (Toronto: Dundurn Press, 1988), pp. 284-6.

3. In a review, signed 'D.W.', of *The Hand-Book of Toronto; Containing Its Climate, Geology, Natural History, Educational Institutions, Courts of Law, Municipal Arrangements, &c. &c.*, by a Member of the Press (Toronto: Lovell and Gibson, 1858), in: *The Canadian Journal of Industry, Science, and Art*, n.s., vol. III (Nov. 1858), p. 502; Wilson was general editor of this, the Canadian Institute's journal. There is more in this vein, later on, in the first local histories (such as Henry Scadding's *Toronto of Old*, 1873).

4. 'Toronto', the (Brockville) *Statesman*, Sat., 21 June 1845 (courtesy of Otto). Likewise the editor of the (Toronto) *Star* 'found ample reason for optimism' in 1844, as quoted in: Eric Arthur, *Toronto, No Mean City*, 3d ed., rev. Stephen A. Otto (Toronto: University of Toronto Press, © 1986), p. 80; the editor of the (Toronto) *Globe* — founded in 1844 — took an annual 'walkabout' to chronicle the city's improvement; Stephen Otto has genereously shared his extensive files of such articles that resulted.

5. Most references to the *Hand-Book of Toronto* (see n. 3 for full citation) are included in the text for economy of space. And, as vitual-

ly all of the buildings mentioned subsequently are discussd (and often illustrated) in standard works on Toronto architecture, the reader should consult these three: Otto/Arthur, *Toronto, No Mean City* (cited in n. 4); William Dendy, *Lost Toronto*, rev. ed. (Toronto: McClelland & Stewart, 1993); William Dendy and William Kilbourn, *Toronto Observed* (Toronto: Oxford University Press, 1986).

6. The author says that it is 'after the design, in a considerably modified sense, of the Crystal Palace of 1851.' Almost identical wording occurs in a reference I owe to Robert Hill: 'The Crystal Palace of Toronto, Canada', *Illustrated London News*, vol. XXXIII (16 Oct. 1858), pp. 363-4. It was cruciform like its prototype, but only 256 by 144 feet (compared with 1848 by 408 feet), and roofed in tin — producing a heavy appearance — instead of the glass that gave the original Crystal Palace its distinctive transparency.

7. For the competition announcement see 'The Provincial Fair in Toronto', (Toronto) *Globe*, Tues., 13 Apr. 1858, p. 2, col. 9, and 'Plans for Provincial Exhibition Building', in the same issue, p. 3, col. 4; the result was announced in 'The Exhibition Building', *Globe*, Tues., 11 May 1858, p. 2, col. 8; according to John Ross Robertson, *Landmarks of Toronto*, vol. 2 (Toronto: Telegram, 1896), p. 1089, there were 13 entries — two of them by Fleming & Schreiber, who took both first and second prizes, and were asked to combine elements from both into one design (all references courtesy of Robert Hill).

8. This summary was based on William Brown's *City Directory* for 1856. On the role of iron in Toronto buildings from the 1850s see John Andre, Stephen Otto, and Douglas Richardson, 'William Kauffmann, 1821/2 – 1875', in: Society for the Study of Architecture in Canada, *Selected Papers*, vol. 5 (1982), especially pp. 51-6 and figs. 1-4. In addition see Dendy, *Lost Toronto*, pp. 24-27.

9. In the Archives of University College, University of Toronto.

10. See Arthur/Otto, *Toronto*, p. 250; entry by Frederick H. Armstrong, s.v. 'Hay, William', in *Dictionary of Canadian Biography*, vol. XI

(© 1982), pp. 391-3; Armstrong, *A City in the Making*, ch. 11, 'An Ambulatory Architect: William Hay', pp. 212-26; and Malcolm Thurlby, s.v. 'Hay, William', in *The Dictionary of Art*, ed. Jane Turner, vol. 14 (New York: Grove, 1996), p. 259.

11. The drawings for the Yorkville Town Hall are in the Langley Collection, Toronto Reference Library. See Dendy, *Lost Toronto*, pp. [206-8], and Anita Makler, 'Coloured Brick in Yorkville', *The Journal of Canadian Art History*, vol. IV, no. 2 (1977-8), pp. 98-110.

12. See W. Stewart Wallace, *The Macmillan Dictionary of Canadian Biography*, 3d ed. (London, etc.: Macmillan, 1963), p. 764. Ure was in Toronto in 1850: he was involved in an incident in the reporters' gallery at the Legislature for which he was publicly reprimanded by the Speaker (unfairly, it seems): see the 80th Anniversary number of the *Globe*, 4 March 1924, and 'One Hundred Years Ago from *The Globe* Files', *Globe and Mail*, 20 July 1950.

13. I am grateful to Luba Frastacky, who suggested that Hay's copy was extra-illustrated; we examined three copies of the *Hand-Book* in Fisher Library at University of Toronto, and records of copies elsewhere.

14. With a different cutline ('The Proposed New General Hospital'), this had accompanied a description of the hospital in 'The Editor's Shanty', *The Anglo-American Magazine*, vol. 4, no. 2 (February 1854), pp. 211-12. It is reproduced in Charles P. de Volpi, *Toronto: A Pictorial Record* (Montreal: Dev-Sco Publications, 1965), pl. 28.

15. The map measures 12 $3/4$ by 22 $3/8$ inches (31.9 by 56.4 cm) between the borders, and lies between p. 272 and the back flyleaf. It is reproduced in de Volpi, *Toronto*, pl. 41.

16. For King's, see Douglas Richardson et al., *A Not Unsightly Building: University College and its History* (Toronto: University College, 1990), especially pp. 11-12 (pl. 2.3), and ch. 3 (pp. 24-47).

17. Reference courtesy of Robert Hill.

18. Developed in 1871-2, by Hay's pupil, Henry Langley: see Douglas

Richardson and Angela K. Carr, s.v. 'Langley, Henry', *Dictionary of Canadian Biography*, vol. XIII (© 1994), p. 575.

19. Morriss, *The Journal of John George Howard*, especially vol. 3, pp. 236 (n. 4) and 244, vol. 4, pp. 156, 161-2 (n. 8), 164, and 182.

20. Yet the *Hand-Book* concludes: 'The grounds were laid out under the superintendence of the late Mr. [David] Mundie, one of our most successful landscape gardeners.' For Mundie see David Bain, 'William Mundie, landscape gard[e]ner', *Journal of Garden History*, vol. 5 (1985), pp. 298-308.

21. For the bank, Dr Baldwin's work, and Howard's additions, see Sheldon Godfrey and Judy Godfrey, *Stones, Bricks, and History: The Corner of "Duke and George", 1798-1984*, [3d] expanded and rev. ed. (Toronto: Lester & Orpen Dennys, © 1984), especially pp. 7-9, 16-17; and Susan Wagg, 'A Critical Look at Bank Architecture', in *Money Matters* (New York: McGraw-Hill, © 1990), pp. 33-4.

22. On Cumberland and the Ridouts, and the bank addition, see Godfrey and Godfrey, *Stones, Bricks, and History*, pp. 21-3; and Geoffrey Simmins, Fred Cumberland: *Building the Victorian Dream* (Toronto: University of Toronto Press, © 1997), pp. 14, 24-5, 184, 192-3, 201-5 (pls. 14.16-14.21), 258, 275.

23. One can visualize McGill Square as a park in a view of the newly built church in Arthur/Otto, *Toronto*, p. [221], pl. 5.101. Similarly, the 7-acre residential park known as St James' Square was acquired by the Province in 1850 for the Normal School (Dendy, *Lost Toronto*, p. 150), and beautified by David Mundie in 1853.

24. Eric Arthur, 'The Nineteenth Century', in: *St Lawrence Hall* (Toronto: Thomas Nelson & Sons, 1969), p. 32. See also Neil Einarson, s.v. 'Thomas, William', in: *Dictionary of Canadian Biography*, vol. VIII (© 1985), pp. 872-8; and Glenn McArthur and Annie Szamosi, *William Thomas, Architect, 1799-1860* (n.p. [Ottawa]: Carleton University Press, © 1996), pp. 25, 48-51.

25. Ridout and Storm should share credit with Cumberland, though Ridout's contribution is undetermined, while Storm was responsi-

ble for much of the draughting. See Shirley Morriss with Carl Benn, 'Architecture', in: *The Parish and Cathedral of St James'* [sic], *Toronto, 1797-1997*, ed. William Cooke (Toronto: Printed for the Cathedral by the University of Toronto Press, © 1998), pp. 194-208; Simmins, *Fred Cumberland*, pp. 124-39, 252-4.

26. Ridout should be credited with Cumberland: see Simmins, *Fred Cumberland*, pp. 88, 90, 255-6.

27. Storm should be credited with Cumberland. See ibid., pp. 168-9, 179, 269-70.

28. Again, both Ridout and Storm should be credited with Cumberland. See ibid., pp. 154-7, 159-60, 261-2.

29. Here Storm's name is mentioned (although officially this, too, should be credited to Cumberland & Ridout). See ibid., pp. 76, [149], 150-1, 261.

30. See standard references; also Andre, Otto and Richardson, 'William Kauffmann', pp. [48]-49, 55-6.

31. It is also neglected by Simmins, *Fred Cumberland*, especially p. 249. But see Ralph Greenhill, Ken Macpherson, and Douglas Richardson, *Ontario Towns* (n.p. [Ottawa]: Oberon, © 1974), pl. 78 and chapter on 'Public Buildings & Schools' (unpaged): a uniform plan for registry offices, drawn up by the (Ontario) Department of Public Works, was approved by Order-in-Council, 9 March 1868, and based (according to Robert Hill) on that at Cobourg by James Smith — which was indebted in turn to Cumberland's registry office in Toronto. See also Richardson, *A Not Unsightly Building*, pp. 83 and 85 (pl. 5.14).

32. Arthur/Otto, *Toronto*, p. 154 (pl. 4.123).

33. For the McCausland firm, see Alice Hamilton and Douglas Richardson, s.v. 'McCausland, Joseph', *Dictionary of Canadian Biography*, vol. XIII (© 1994), pp. 612-13. This early glass by McCausland is conventional Gothic Revival work: many symbolic motifs (a chalice, the pelican in her piety, etc.) set in traditional fields (such as a quatrefoil, or a mandorla, etc.) and symmetrically distributed with tapestry-like effect.

34. The actual appearance of St Basil's and St Michael's at the time is

shown in a photograph, c. 1870 (when the complex was still little changed), in Richardson, *A Not Unsightly Building*, p. 58 (pl. 4.11).

35. See Richardson, *A Not Unsightly Building*, passim.

36. For Osgoode, see Simmins, *Fred Cumberland*, pp. 160-9, 173-4, 177-8, 277-9. On the exhibition of drawings, see *Transactions of the Board of Agriculture* (1858), p. 197, which lists the firm as taking first and second prizes for architectural perspectives shown at the Provincial Exhibition (reference courtesy of Mary Allodi). Drawings in the Horwood Collection, Ontario Archives, on Whatman's heavy Turkey Mill watercolour paper bearing dated watermarks suggest that Osgoode Hall and St James' Cathedral were two of the subjects; it is likely that Edinburgh Assurance, constructed in 1858, was also exhibited.

37. For the Rossin House, see Andre, Otto, and Richardson, 'William Kauffmann', especially pp. 52-4.

38. The tender call appeared in (Toronto) *Globe*, 4 Nov. 1857, p. 3 (reference courtesy of Stephen A. Otto). See also Robertson, *Landmarks of Toronto*, vol. 4, pp. 29-32, 582.

39. Hay & Gundry's successor, Henry Langley, produced a distinguished example that survives — St Thomas' (Anglican) Church, Brooklin, of 1869 — for which see Greenhill, Macpherson, and Richardson, *Ontario Towns*, pl. 54 and chapter on 'Meeting Houses & Churches' (unpaged), where I provide references to an important source and to my own detailed treatment of gothic churches in wood.

40. *The City of Toronto: Illustrated by Oil-Colour Views taken from Photographs*, Nelson and Sons' Hand-Books (Toronto: James Campbell, 1860), pp. 12-13. The book is available on microfiche from the Canadian Institute for Historical Microreproductions (CIHM no. 48690). It is attributed by CIHM to John George Hodgins — for reasons that are unclear — but Robert Stacey (who brought the book to Stephen Otto's attention, and mine) suggests that Daniel Wilson is a more likely candidate. Wilson was a friend of the publisher, Thomas Nelson. Reviewing Ure's book (guarded-

ly) — see n. 3 — he was aware of Ure's shortcomings, and had the requisite talents for the task himself.

41. I have given an account of these elsewhere: Douglas Richardson, 'The Original Building and Its Architect', in: George Baird et al., '999 Queen: A Case Study of Government Demolition', *The Second City Book*, eds. James Lorimer and Evelyn Ross (Toronto: James Lorimer & Co., 1977), pp. 81-5 (others' contributions extend coverage to pp. 70-95).

42. Joseph Chandler (from Girard College Building Committee's *Final Report)*, quoted in: Bates Lowry, *Building a National Image: Architectural Drawings for the American Democracy, 1789-1912* (Washington, D.C.: National Building Museum; New York: Walker, © 1985), p. 41.

CHAPTER 3 SUBJECT TO CHANGE: ASYLUM LANDSCAPE
by Pleasance Crawford

1. *The City and the Asylum* (Toronto: The Museum of Mental Health Services (Toronto) Inc., 1993), 'Mississauga Indian Land Claim,' p. 32.

2. National Archives of Canada (NAC), National Map Collection, #17026, 'Plan of York Surveyed and Drawn by Lieut Phillpotts Royal Engineers, May 24, 1818,' reproduced in R.L. Gentilcore and C.G. Head, *Ontario's History in Maps* (Toronto: University of Toronto Press, 1984), p. 252.

3. Toronto Reference Library (TRL), Special Collections, copy, 'R.E. Office, Toronto, 20th Feb 1835.'

4. 'The Insane. Present Population of the Toronto Asylum,' *The Globe*, Toronto, Jan. 2, 1884.

5. TRL, John G. Howard (JGH) Papers, L 27, Plan of Asylum Grounds, May 1845; and Archives for the History of Canadian Psychiatry and Mental Health Services (AHCPMHS), Ian Wheal, 'Lands of Provincial Lunatic Asylum and Asylum Farm,' Typescript, July 1999, pp. 1-2.

6. AO, RG 10, MS 640, 20-B-5, v. 2, [Commissioners'] Minute Book, June 13, Aug. 1, and Aug. 8, 1846.

7. NAC, Picture Division, #C-13428, 'Insane Asylum, Toronto, Canadawest [sic]'; reproduced in Edith G. Firth, *Toronto in Art* (Toronto: Fitzhenry & Whiteside, 1983), pp. 24-25.

8. AO, RG 10, MS 640, 20-B-4, v. 6, [Daniel Clark's] Journal, Dec. 31, 1878 and May 1, 1879.

9. TRL, JGH Papers, III, L 27, Box 2-2, JGH to Commissioners, report on PLA, n.d.; and JGH to Commissioners, office copy of letter written Jan. 8, 1848.

10. TRL, Repro T 10966, reproduced in William Dendy. *Lost Toronto* (Toronto: McClelland & Stewart, 1993), p. 164; AHCPMHS, 'Main Building, Toronto,' reproduced in annual reports for 1910 and 1911.

11. 'Special Report of Mr. Taché,' Annual Report of the Board of Inspectors . . . for the year 1860.

12. AHCPMHS, Wheal, pp. 1-2.

13. AO, [Commissioners'] Minute Book, Oct.1845 through Jan. 1847.

14. 'Provincial Lunatic Asylum . . . Tenders are required . . . Cumberland & Ridout,' *The Daily Globe*, June 28, 1851, p.1, c.6.

15. AO, RG 15, Ser. E-4, v. 11, #1, office copy of letter, Kivas Tully to Joseph Workman, Feb. 18, 1860, to accompany AO, RG 15-13-2-41, 'P.L. Asylum. Details of Boundary Wall . . . Feb. 18, 1860.'

16. Several of Daniel Clark's annual reports referred to this event (although his figures varied over the years). See, for example, Annual reports of the Medical Superintendent for the years ending Sept. 30, 1888, 1889, and 1904.

17. Annual reports of the Medical Superintendent for the years ending Sept. 30, 1890 and 1896; and AO, RG 15, Ser. E-1, Box 17-7, Miscellaneous statements and reports 1868-91, 'Map of the Lunatic Asylum Toronto,' [Dec. 1891].

18. AO, RG 10, MS 640, 20-B-4, v. 6, [Daniel Clark's] Journal, June 11, July 10, and Aug. 28, 1878; and AO, RG 15-13-2-51, Job #411, BP-3, K-539, 'Detail for Gate—Superintendent's Residence,' n.d.

19. AO, RG 15-13-2-1335, Job #634, L-211; and AO, RG 15-13-2, Job #411, BP3-21, L-211.

20. AO, [Commissioners'] Minute Book, June 13 and July 4, 1846.
21. TRL, JGH Papers, III, L 27, Box 2-2, JGH to Commissioners, office copy of letter written Jan. 8, 1848.
22. I am grateful to Shirley Morriss for this information from Howard's journal for 1850. The plan itself has not been found.
23. Annual reports of the Medical Superintendent for the years ending Nov. 1, 1850 and 1851.
24. Annual Reports of the Medical Superintendent for the year 1867-68.
25. TRL, JGH Papers, III, L 27, Box 2-2, JGH to Commissioners, office copy of letter written Jan. 8, 1848.
26. Annual reports of the Medical Superintendent for the years ending Nov. 1, 1851 and 1854.
27. Annual Report of the Medical Superintendent for the year ending Sept. 30, 1877.
28. Annual reports of the Medical Superintendent for the years ending Sept. 30, 1877, 1897, and 1904, and Nov. 1, 1910.
29. Annual Report of the Medical Superintendent for the year ending Nov. 1, 1852; and Annual Report of the Inspector for 1863.
30. AO, RG 10, MS 640, 20-B-4, v. 6, [Daniel Clark's] Journal, Oct. 29, 1878; and table entitled 'Return of Farm and Garden Produce,' which was appended to the annual reports from at least 1893 through 1905. The table listed the quantities of vegetables, milk, eggs, bedding plants, bulbs, and flower seeds produced each year, and assigned a market value to each line item. Annual totals were in the $5500 to $7000 range.
31. Annual Report of of the Medical Superintendent for the year ending Sept. 30, 1876.
32. Annual Report of the Medical Superintendent for the year ending Oct. 31, 1918. For a detailed account of the use of patients as workers, see AHCPMHS, Geoffrey F. Reaume, *999 Queen Street West: Patient Life at the Toronto Hospital for the Insane, 1870-1940*, Ph.D. thesis, Graduate Dept. of History, University of Toronto, 1997, ch. 5, 'Patients' Labour.'
33. Ontario Dept. of Health, Hospitals Branch, Annual Report on the Toronto Hospital for 1949.

34. Annual reports of the Medical Superintendent for the years 1857 and 1862; and AHCPMHS, Wheal, 2, 12 (n. 23). Daniel Clark's annual report for 1870-71 refers to the expiry of the lease to the "Bacon Farm." The exact location of this land merits further research.

35. Annual Report of the Inspector . . . for 1868-69.

36. Annual Report of the Inspector . . . for 1869-70; Annual reports of the Medical Superintendent for for 1869-70 and 1870-71.

37. AO, RG 10, MS 640, 20-B-4, v. 6, [Daniel Clark's] Journal, June 12, 1878, and Dec. 31, 1878; 'Civic Affairs. Exhibition Committee,' and 'The City Council,' *The Globe*, Toronto, Dec. 31, 1878, p. 2, c.5 and p.4, c.7 respectively.

38. 'Farm,' Annual Report of the Medical Superintendent for the year ending Sept. 30, 1892.

39. AO, [Commissioners'] Minute Book, Oct. 13, 1849.

40. First Annual Report of the Directors of the Provincial Lunatic Asylum for the year 1850.

41. Annual Report of the Medical Superintendent for the year ending Nov. 1, 1851.

42. AHCPMHS, Emily Hopewell, 'Memoires of My Office Career at the Ontario Hospitals, New Toronto, Woodstock, Toronto, 1930-1968,' typescript, n.d. [1968?], p. 8.

43. AO, RG 15-13-2-1329, L-211, 'Plan Showing Elevations Ontario Hosptial Grounds . . .,' Oct. 31, 1961.

44. TRL, Special Collections, Toronto: Its Buildings, Grounds, and Places of Interest . . . (Toronto: Hart & Rawlinson, 1878), p. 14 (photocopy in file at AHCPMHS).

45. For information on patients' leisure activities, see the annual reports on the institution, Daniel Clark's journals, and Reaume, ch. 4, 'Patients' Leisure and Personal Space.'

46. AO, RG 15, Ser. E-1, v. 29, #, and Ser. V-2. v. 4]; and AO, RG 15-13-2-41, #411, BP-3, K-539, 'P.L. Asylum.—Design for Fountain . . . , Aug. 12, 1859.'

47. Fern Bayer, *The Ontario Collection* (Markham, ON: Fitzhenry & Whiteside, 1984), pp. 291, 364-65; and telephone conversation

with Irma Ditchburn, 25 January 2000.

48. For information on recent plantings and other landscape elements I am grateful to John Court, Steven Hughes, and Martin Rudd.

49. On-site interview and walkabout with Steven Hughes and Martin Rudd, 29 December 1999.

50. Kathryn Anderson, 'Provincial Lunatic Asylum Walls, 1001 Queen Street West,' Heritage Property Report, Toronto Historical Board, September 1996.

51. On-site interview and walkabout with Steven Hughes and Martin Rudd, 29 December 1999.

CHAPTER 4   BUILDING CANADA WEST
by Alec Keefer

1. Richard Wagner, quoted in 'Essay on The Story', by H. E.Krehbiel, in: *La Sonnambula*, 1831, editor Felice Romani (New York: G.Schirmer,1929), p viii

2. Natalia MacFarren, 'The English Version' in: *La Sonnambula*, 1831, editor Felice Romani (New York: G.Schirmer,1929), pp. 193-200.

3. H. E. Krehbiel, 'Essay on The Story', in: *La Sonnambula*, 1831. editor Felice Romani, (New York: G.Schirmer, 1929), p. xi

4. R. E. Zegger, *John Cam Hobhouse: A Political Life, 1819-1852*, (Columbia: University of Missouri Press,1973), p.157

5. James Elmes and T. H. Shepherd, *Metropolitan Improvements; or, London in the Nineteenth Century*, (London:1829.)

6. Rev. John Keble, 'New Every Morning Is The Love', in: *The Book of Common Praise.*(London: 1821), p. 2

7. Raymond Williams, *Culture and Society: 1780-1950.* (London:Chattos and Windos, 1958), p. 68

8. Hermione Hobhouse, *A History of Regent Street,* (London: Macdonald and Jane's, in association with Queen Anne Press, 1975), p. 19.

9. William Hogarth, *Analysis of Beauty*, (London:1753).

10. Van Zanten, *Designing Paris: The Architecture of Duban,*

Labrouste, Duc, and Vaudoyer, (Cambridge: The MIT Press 1987), p xiii.

11. *ibid*, p. 246

12. *ibid*

13. For a description of the idealism of the 1830's and 1840's see: Harvey Stalwick, *A History of Asylum Administration in Canada before Confederation*. Ph.D. thesis, University of London, U.K., 1969 p. 206. and for further comments see: Thomas Brown, *Living with God's Afflicted*, Ph.D. thesis, Queen's University, Kingston, On., 1980. p.5-11

14. Photography is generally considered to have originated with the colloidal chemical process in 1839. The *camera obscura* and *camera lucida* were known and used by some interested artists from the fifteenth century, but not architects because their task is to draw something that does not yet exist.

15. J. Russell Harper, *Painting in Canada - a history* (Toronto: University of Toronto Press et les Presses de l'universite Laval, 1966), p. 42

16. Gavin Stamp, *The Great Perspectivists* (New York: Rizzoli International Publications Inc., 1982), pp 12-16

17. John Berger, *Ways of Seeing* (London: BBC and Penguin Books, 1972), p. 16

18. Gavin Stamp *op. cit.*, p.7

19. Carolyn Young, *The Glory of Ottawa* (Canada: McGill-Queen's University Press, 1995), chapter 2

20. Gavin Stamp, *op. cit* as note 16. for a long and interesting discussion of this point. Also see R. Myerscough-Walker *The Perspectivist* (London: Sir Isaac Pitman & Sons, Ltd.,1958)

CHAPTER 5 JOHN GEORGE HOWARD ARCHITECT
by Shirley Morriss

1. Entry by Edith G. Firth, 'Howard, John George.', in *Dictionary of Canadian Biography*, Vol. XI (Toronto: University of Toronto

Press, 1982) pp. 426-428. For a daily record of Howard's activities see [John George Howard] *The Journal of John George Howard 1833-49* ed. Shirley G. Morriss, 7 vols in 3(Toronto: Ontario Heritage Foundation, n.d. [1987]). See also Shirley McManus, *The Life of John George Howard.* (THB, 1975). The original journals (1833-86), as well as drawings, plans, and related papers are held by the Toronto Reference Library, the Archives of Ontario, and Heritage Toronto.

2. Sharon Vattay, 'John Howard, the UCC drawing master who shaped Toronto,' *Old Times* (Summer 1997), pp. 12-15

3. Howard's work for the city can be traced in the City of Toronto Council Minutes and Cartographic Records Collection.

4. See OMNR: Survey Records, #PLS6477 P10-22, for Howard's chart and map of the Toronto Harbour, 17 Aug. 1846. See also CTA: SC 206, for his report of the survey of the Toronto Harbour and TRL: L27, 1370, 1373, Notebooks 9 and 10 and Box 1, Folders 3 and 7.

5. Edith G. Firth, *The Town of York, 1815 - 1834,* (Toronto: University of Toronto Press, Champlain Society for the Government of Ontario, 1966), p. 82

6. William Dendy, *Lost Toronto: Images of the City's Past* 2nd ed. (Toronto: McClelland & Stewart, 1993), pp. 95-6

7. Leslie Maitland, *Neoclassical Architecture in Canada* (Ottawa: National Historic Parks and Sites Branch, Parks Canada, 1984), p. 57

8. Marion MacRae & Anthony Adamson, *The Ancestral Roof: domestic architecture of Upper Canada* (Toronto: Clarke, Irwin & Company Limited, 1963), pp. 87-94

9. Eric Arthur, *Toronto No Mean City* 3rd ed., rev. Stephen A. Otto (Toronto: University of Toronto press, 1986), p. 109

10. Mathilde Brosseau, *Gothic Revival in Canadian Architecture* (Ottawa: National Historic Parks and Sites Branch, Parks Canada, 1980), pp. 108-9

11. Marion MacRae and Anthony Adamson, *Hallowed Walls: church architecture of Upper Canada* (Toronto: Clarke Irwin, 1975), pp.

85-103. See also Ralph Greenhill, Ken MacPherson and Douglas Richardson, *Ontario Towns* (n.p.[Ottawa]: Oberon, 1974), [pp. 23-4] and pl. 26.

12. Harold Kalman, *A History of Canadian Architecture*, 2 vols (Toronto: Oxford University Press; 1994), I: p. 272-3.

13. William Cooke, gen. ed., *The Parish and Cathedral Church of St. James, Toronto, 1797-1997* (Toronto: St. James' Cathedral, 1998), pp. 214-15.

14. Marion MacRae & Anthony Adamson, *Cornerstones of Order: courthouses and town halls of Ontario 1784-1914* (Toronto: Clarke Irwin, 1983), pp. 59-62

15. NAC, RG 5, C-1, vol. 133, file 8186, Canada West, Provincial Secretary's Office, Numbered Correspondence, 3 Aug. 1844.

16. AO, RG 10, MS640, Series 20-B5, Records of the commissioners, vol. 2, Minute Book, 1844 - 1850, 3 Dec. 1844. See also Morriss, *Journal,* vol. 4; 5, 11, and 14 Dec. 1844

17. *Statutes of Upper Canada*, 2 Vict, Chap 11, 1839,pp 32-36.

18. AO: RG 10, MS 640, Series 20-B5 Records of the Commissioners, Vol. 3, Letter Book 1839-49, W.H.Boulton to Col. Halloway, 26 May and W.H.Boulton to D.Daly, 9 June 1845

19. Records of the Commissioners, Minute Book, 26 May and 7 June 1845; see also AO: RG 15, 12-0-16, No. 4 and 13-2-40, Job No. 411 A1-1, no. 28.

20. Records of the Commissioners, Minute Book, 14 Feb. - 23 May 1846.

21. *British Colonist*, 25 Aug. 1846

22. QSMHC, John G Howard to the Chairman of the Commission for erecting the Provincial Lunatic Asylum, 20 Mar. 1847. See CTA, Toronto City Council Minutes, 17 April 1848.

23. Morriss, *Journal,* vol. 5; 7 June 1845

24. TRL: Howard Papers, L27, Box II, folder2.

25. Morriss, *Journal*, vol. 3; 2 and 3 Feb. 1841

26. Three catalogues document the activities of the local artists: *Catalogue of the First Exhibition of the Society of Artists & Amateurs of Toronto,* (Toronto, 1834); *Toronto Society of Arts: First Exhibition, 1847*, (Toronto?,

1847?); and,

Toronto Society of Arts: Second Exhibition, 1848, (Toronto?, 1848?)

27. J.G.H. 'The Tomb in High Park,' 1877 *Catalogue of Paintings in the Gallery at Colborne Lodge, High Park* . . . (Toronto, 1885) p. 11

28. E.B. Shuttleworth, *The Windmill* (Toronto: W.G.Gooderham, 1924)

CHAPTER 6 HOWARD VS TULLY: A CONTRAST AND COMPARISON OF THE PROPOSED DESIGN VS. THE AS-BUILT DESIGN FOR THE EAST AND WEST WINGS OF THE PROVINCIAL LUNATIC ASYLUM
by Steven Bell

1. Sir Banister Fletcher, *A History of Architecture*. Edited by John Musgrove. 19th edition (London: Butterworths, 1987)

2. John Blumenson, *Ontario Architecture: A Guide to Styles and Building Terms 1784 to the present*. 2nd edition (Markham, Ontario: Fitzhenry & Whiteside, 1990)

3. Paul Spencer Byard, *The Architecture of Additions - Design and Regulation*. (New York: W.W. Norton & Company, 1998)

4. William Dendy, *Lost Toronto,* rev ed. (Toronto: McClelland & Stewart, 1993)

5. Jan Gympel, *The story of architecture: from antiquity to the present* (Köln: Könemann Verlagsgesellchaft mbH, 1996).

6. Thomas Markins, *Architecture As Therapy*

7. Harry Mayerovitch, *How architecture speaks - and fashions our lives* (Montreal: Robert Davies Publishing, 1996)

8. Archives of Ontario Special Collections

9. Ontario Hospital — 999 Queen Street West, John George Howard Architectural Drawings for the Provincial Lunatic Asylum.

10. Ontario Hospital — 999 Queen Street West, Kivas Tully Architectural Drawings for the Provincial Lunatic Asylum. Reference: RG 13-2-42; RG 15-13-2-40; RG 15-13-2-46.

Sessional Papers. Legislature of Ontario. 1866 -1875
Inspector's Reports and Superintendent's Reports

CHAPTER 7 JOSEPH WORKMAN, ASYLUM SUPERINTENDENT
by Christine Johnston

1. *The* (Toronto) *Globe*, Feb. 11, 19, 24; March 2; April 25; May 12, 1857
2. Dr. Hake Tuke, *The Insane in the United States and Canada*, (London: 1885) p.216 and
    Donald Jones, 'Toronto Merchant becomes Father of Canadian Psychiatry,' *Toronto Star*,May 2, 1981
3. See *Globe*, 1857
4. Chris Raible, 'Case History/Notes et dossiers de recherche. 'Your Daughter & I Are Not Likely To Quarrel': Notes on a dispute between Joseph Workman and William Lyon Mackenzie.' *Canadian Bulletin of Medical History* 11:2(1994),p. 387-395
5. Dr. J. Workman, 'Proceedings of the Thirteenth Annual Meeting of the Association of Medical Superintendents of American Institutions for the Insane,' *American Journal of Insanity* 15 (July, 1858),p.80.
6. Dr. C. K. Clarke, Letter to Workman on the occasion of his eighty-seventh birthday, May 26, 1892.
7. Dr. J. Workman, 'Address to students 1883,' (Matrix collection at the Queen Street Mental Health Centre, repro. in 1980 for the opening of the Joseph Workman Auditorium.)
8. H. E. MacDermot, *One Hundred Years of Medicine in Canada, 1867-1967*, (Toronto:1967),pp. 36-37

The three journals kept by Workman are:
Asylum Journals 1872-1875, (Academy of Medicine Collection, Thomas Fisher Rare Book Library, University of Toronto Library).
   Personal Diaries 1867-1894, (University of Toronto Archives, with typed excerpts in the Academy of Medicine Collection, Thomas Fisher Rare Book Library, University of Toronto).
   Weather Journals 1860-1894, (Library of Environment Canada, Toronto).

1.   Kathryn McPherson, *Bedside Matters: The Transformation of Canadian Nursing, 1900-1990,* (Toronto: Oxford University Press, 1996), p. 30

2.   ibid, p. 39

3.   C.K.Clarke, Annual Report of the Medical Superintendent for the Asylum for the Insane, Toronto, Ontario, for the year ending 30 September 1905. In the Thirty-eighth Annual Report of the Inspector of Prisons and Public Charities (Toronto: King's Printer, 1906)

4.   R.W.Bruce-Smith, 'Training Schools for Asylum Nurses in Ontario', *The Canadian Nurse* 2 (4): 23 (1906)

5.   Gifford C.Price, *A History of the Ontario Hospital, Toronto,* Unpublished Thesis, School of Social Work, University of Toronto, 1950, p. 66

6.   C.K.Clarke, Annual Report of Medical Superintendent...for...1906 (Toronto: King's Printer, 1907)

7.   The lack of precise labelling on the archival negative makes a positive identification difffficult. The general dating, however, does support that these young women were among the first students to attend the Training School. The photographer's name, unfortunately, is unrecorded. The earliest mention of students that successfully completed the program is in the 1907 Annual Report.

8.   Dr C.K.Clarke was a prominent and vocal proponent of the 'science' of eugenics and Social Darwinism. This has served to qualify his stature as a progressive reformer. See: Ian Dowbiggin, *Keeping America Sane: Psychiatry and Eugenics in the United States and Canada, 1880-1940,* (Ithaca, N.Y.: Cornell University Press, 1997)

9.   Dr. Charles Sheard and Dr. Charles Hastings in Public Health were part of this progressive reform. See: Paul Rutherford, editor, *Saving the City: the First Phase 1880-1920.* (Toronto: University

of Toronto Press, 1974), pp. 124-136

10.   Cyril Greenland, *Charles Kirk Clarke: A pioneer of Canadian psychiatry* (Toronto: The Clarke Institute of Psychiatry, 1966), p. 9

11.   R.W.Bruce-Smith, op. cit.

12.   C.K.Clarke, 'Some Remarks upon the Nursing of Cases of Mental Disease', *The Canadian Nurse* 2 (3): pp. 11-14 (1906)

13.   Edwin R.Rogers, Inspector of Lunatics and Idiot Asylums, included this recommendation for a name change in his 1906 report: 'the modern tendency is to do away with the name *Asylum* in connection with Institutions for the care of the insane. Both in Europe and United States the term *Asylum* for the *Insane* is rapidly becoming obsolete. When such institutions were looked upon as mere places of custody and safety, the name was not inappropriate but since medical treatment has become a prominent feature it is evident that the term *Hospital* is the proper designation for such an organization.' E.R.Rogers, Introductory Remarks, in thirty-eighth Annual report of the Inspector of Prisons and public Charities...for the year ending 30 September 1905. (Toronto: King's printer, 1906)

14.   A further change occured in 1919 when 'for the Insane' was dropped from the name of the provincial hospitals. They became simply 'Ontario Hospitals' See Gifford C.Price, op. cit.., pp. 112, 125

15   J.M.Forster, 'Annual Report of the Medical Superintendent of the Hospital for the Insane, Toronto, Ontario, for the year ending 31 October 1911', in Forty-fourth Annual Report of the Inspector of Prisons and Public Charities...(Toronto: King's printer, 1912). The last fully integrated and in-house training program for both men and women was the Psychiatric Nursing Assistants program that operated out of the Queen Street Mental Health Centre between 1969 and 1974. Centre hi-lites (QSMHC newsletter) Fall 1974. Courtesy AHCP&MHS.

16.   Nurse historian Margaret L. Gorrie writes, 'Women who were seen to excel in nursing were often described in terms of their character traits. They might be understanding, patient, tactful, versatile, and interesting.' Margaret L. Gorrie, 'Nursing', in Edward Shorter,

editor, *TPH: History and memories of the Toronto Psychiatric Hospital, 1925-1966*, (Toronto: Wall & Emerson, Inc., 1996), p. 194

17. Edward Ryan, 'The Relation of the work of Hospitals for the Insane to that of General Hospitals,' *The Canadian Nurse* 3(5): pp. 251-253 (1907)

18. C.K.Clarke, 'Some Remarks Upon the Nursing of Cases of Mental Disease', op. cit., p. 11

19. C.K.Clarke, Report of the Medical Superintendent...for...1906

20. C.K.Clarke, as n. 18

21. M. Patricia Donahue, *Nursing, The Finest Art, an Illustrated History* (Toronto: The C.V.Mosby Co., 1985), p. 325

22. Margaret L. Gorrie, op. cit., p. 196

23. The City and the Asylum: Celebrating the Bi-Centennial of the City of Toronto, 1793-1993 (Toronto: The Museum of Mental Health Services (Toronto) Inc., 1993), p. 16

24. Kathryn McPherson, op. cit., p.38

25. Cyril Greenland, 'A Revealing Portrait of Dr. C.K.Clarke', *Ontario Medical Review*, Nov. 1980, p. 581

CHAPTER 10 FROM 999 TO 1001 QUEEN STREET:
A CONSISTENTLY VITAL RESOURCE
by John Court

1. Archives for the History of Canadian Psychiatry and Mental Health Services (AHCPMHS), Centre for Addiction and Mental Health, Toronto: Drs. S.W. Hamilton and G.A. Kempf, *A Survey of the Ontario Hospitals.* (New York: Mental Hospital Survey Committee, February 1937), 17, 58, 13.

2. AHCPMHS: *Report of the Ontario Health Survey Committee [Davis Committee],* Vol. 1, p. 110, 124 and Tables B9 to B11. Toronto: Report to the Minister of Health for Ontario, 3 vols., 1950, re-issued in one vol. by the Minister in 1952.

3. AHCPMHS, Queen Street Ephemera: F.W. Sneddon, M.D., Inspector, Ontario Hospitals, *Report of Visit to Ontario Hospital Toronto, Sept. 6th and 7th, 1956,* report copy, 9.

4. Eric R. Arthur et al., *A Guide to Hospital Building in Ontario: Report of the Committee on Designing, Constructing and Equipping of Public Hospitals in Ontario.* (Toronto: University of Toronto Press for the Ontario Minister of Health, 1954).

5. Archives of Ontario (AO): Dept of Public Works, Ontario, *Plan Showing Elevations, Ontario Hospital Grounds Toronto,* 31 October 1961; RG 15-13-2-1329, L-211. Also ref. photos from that era, e.g. 'New Administration Building, 999 Queen Street W., Toronto' in *Canadian Hospital: Journal of the Canadian Hospital Association,* 37:2 (Feb. 1960), p. 34.

6. AHCPMHS: Dr. Burdett H. McNeel Fonds, 'Care of the Mentally Ill,' typescript signed 'BH McNeel' dated 1958, Psychiatry – History file, Box 2.

7. B.H. McNeel, M.D. and C.H. Lewis, M.D., 'Care of the Mentally Ill in Ontario: History of Treatment, Part 2' in *Canadian Hospital,* 37:3 (March 1960), 48.

8. Sam Sussman, interview with Dr. H.W. Henderson, in *Pioneers of Mental Health and Social Change, 1930 – 1989.* (London, Ont.: Third Eye Publications, ©1989), pp. 67-70

9. AHCPMHS, Queen Street Collection: Henry B. Durost, M.D.,

'Historical Influences and the Mental Hospital,' typescript, February 1973; interview with Dr. A.L. Swanson in *The Automated Hospital*, 2:1, marketing periodical publ. by Amsco Canada Ltd., 1972.

10. B.H. McNeel, M.D. and C.H. Lewis, M.D., 'Care of the Mentally Ill in Ontario: History of Treatment, Part 1' in *Canadian Hospital*, 37:2 (Feb. 1960), 102.

11. H.W. Henderson, M.D., 'Community Services,' in *Canadian Hospital*, 37:2 (Feb. 1960), 51, 50.

12. AHCPMHS, Dr. H.W. Henderson Fonds: staff briefing note, 'Recommendations — Mental Health Facilities', 1 March 1961.

13. Ontario, Minister of Health, *Proposed Revision of Mental Health Program in Ontario*, Report by the Hon. Matthew B. Dymond to the Legislature, January 1959. Cyril Greenland credits Dr. McNeel with having written this report in: Sam Sussman, Interview with Dr. Cyril Greenland, in *Pioneers of Mental Health and Social Change, 1930 – 1989, op. cit.*, p. 119.

14. Minister of Health, *ibid.*, p. 4. Also ref. Sam Sussman, Interview with Dr. John D.M. Griffin, in *Pioneers of Mental Health and Social Change, 1930 – 1989, op. cit.*, pp. 53-4.

15. AHCPMHS, McNeel Fonds: memoranda to the Hon. M.B. Dymond from McNeel, 17 October 1960 and 24 November 1961; letter from McNeel to Mr. Edward Dunlop, 16 October 1961.

16. *Ibid.*: McNeel, *Program, Mental Health Branch, 1962 – 1967*, typescript report, 8 June 1962; Department of Public Works, *Interview Report* (memorandum of OHT project meeting), 8 August 1962.

17. AO Library: Ontario, Department of Health, Annual Report, 1964, p. 71 and 1966, p. 49. Bill Hughey, AO's Senior Health Portfolio Archivist, kindly located these references and others that followed during the 1960s.

18. AHCPMHS, Henderson Fonds: R.W. Ian Urquhart, M.A., M.D., LL.D., *A Study of the Function and Operation of the Mental Health Branch and the Ontario Hospitals*, Report to the Ontario Minister of Health, December 1965 (signed & numbered copy no. 10), pp. 32-3.

19. ibid; also H.W. Henderson, M.D., C.M., 'The Changing Responsibility of Government in the Care and Treatment of he Mentally Ill,' delivered to the Annual Meeting, Canadian Psychiatric Association, June 17, 1967, 4.

20. Paul King, 'Mad Harry Then: Inside Nine Ninety-nine,' in Toronto Life, 3:1, November 1968, p. 72.
Editor's note: The use of 999 as the numeric municipal and postal address for the institution does not appear until after 1921, before then it was not numbered. There was quite a stretch of numbers to choose from, and we have found no explanation for the selection made, written at the time.
Possible origins are many. Those familiar with the Bible, will recall that the good shepherd 'rejoiceth more of that (one found) sheep than of the ninety and nine who went not astray' *Mathew 18;13* Also in *Mark 5:9*, Christ asked of one possessed of an unclean spirit "What is thy name?' He answered 'My name is Legion: for we are many'.' As well see *Revelations 13;18*, where 666 is 'the number of the beast'. The paragraph describes the multiple appearances of followers of the beast (the devil).

21. Kelner *et al.* (1972), *op. cit.*, p. 21. F.H. Kahan, *Brains and Bricks: The History of the Yorkton Psychiatric Centre.* (Regina: White Cross Publications (Saskatchewan CMHA), 1965).

22. AHCPMHS, Queen Street Collection: *The Automated Hospital*, 1972, *op. cit.*

23. Erving Goffman, *Asylums: Essays on the Social Situation of Mental Patients and Other Inmates.* (Garden City, N.Y.: Anchor Books, 1961)

24. Merrijoy J. Kelner et al., 'Feedback: Queen Street Mental Health Centre: Spaces and People,' in *The Canadian Architect*, 20:9, Sept. 1975, pp. 34-40. Also ref. M.J. Kelner, Mary Haour, John P.M. Court and Peter K. New, *Environment and Mental Health: The Effects of the Move to New Treatment Facilities at Queen Street Mental Health Centre.* Toronto: University of Toronto, Interim Report to the Ontario Ministry of Health, December 1972, p. 37.

25. Merrijoy J. Kelner, Mary Haour, John P.M. Court and George Voineskos, 'Environment and Mental Health: the Impact of New Buildings on the Programs and Organization of a Psychiatric Hospital,' in *Canadian Rev. of Sociology & Anthropology*, 12:2, May 1975, pp. 193-205.

26. Kelner et al. (1972), *op. cit.*, p. 56.

27. A.J. Diamond Associates, *Howard Building Feasibility Study*, November 1975, reported and analyzed in: George Baird, research by Robert Hill, '999 Queen: A Collective Failure of Imagination,' in *City Magazine*, 2:3 & 4 (Summer 1976), pp. 34 - 59.

28. AHCPMHS, Queen Street Ephemera: interview with Dr. A.L. Swanson in *The Automated Hospital, op. cit.*, p. 4.

29. Harvey G. Simmons, *Unbalanced: Mental Health Policy in Ontario, 1930 – 1989* (Toronto: Wall & Thompson, ©1990), p. 253; also refer to his analysis of the 1970-89 era, chapters 8-14.

30. Metropolitan Toronto District Health Council, *Directions for Change: Toward a Coordinated Hospital System for Metro Toronto – Final Report of the MTDHC Hospital Restructuring Committee.* Toronto: DHC publication, September 1995, pp. 142-5.

31. See Simmons, *op. cit.*, pp. 169-70, 189-91, 252.

32. Centre for Addiction and Mental Health, *Annual Report to the Community, 1998-99*, p. 2.

33. 'News from the Centre,' in *The Journal of Addiction and Mental Health*, 2:6, Nov./Dec. 1999, p. 2.

CHAPTER 11 ASYLUM LAYOUTS
by Edna Hudson

1. Bill Hillier, *Space is the Machine* (Cambridge: University Press, 1996).

2. John Connolly, M.D., *The Construction & Government of Lunatic Asylums* First published 1847, (London: Dawsons of Pall Mall, reprint 1968)

3. Military considerations probably affected locations of buildings as well. A thorough search of colonial office and other documents remains to be done see: G. Raudzens, *British Ordnance Department and Canada's Canals.* (Waterloo, On: Wilfrid Laurier Press, 1979).

4. John Connolly op. cit., p 42 (Connolly claims his patients at Hanwell use 40 gallons of water per diem)

5. ibid, p10

6. Edna Hudson, *The Romanesque Head Office* (Toronto: Toronto Region Architectural Conservancy, © 1997), chapter 7 and especially chapter 8.

7. Gareth Morgan, *Images of Organization* (Beverly Hills, California: Sage Publications, 1986), pp. 212-214

8. Bill Hillier, *Space is the Machine* (Cambridge: University Press, 1996), pp 211-212

9. See John Sewell papers, City of Toronto Archives

10. G. Baird, '999 Queen Street: A Collective Failure of the Imagination', *City Magazine* 2 (3 and 4), 1976

CONTRIBUTORS

Steven Bell B.A. Architectural Researcher, Culture Division of City of Toronto

William H. Brown, R.N., M.A. is the Infection Control practitioner at the Centre for Addiction and Mental health. He is also a Ph. D. candidate at Ontario Institute for Studies in Education at the University of Toronto, and is interested in the uses of photography in historical research.

John P.M. Court, M.A. is an independent historian and the Archivist of the Archives for the History of Canadian Psychiatry and Mental Health Services (AHCP&MHS) located at the Queen Street Site of the Centre for Addiction and Mental Health, Toronto.

Pleasance Kaufman Crawford is a landscape design historian, interested in many types of cultural landscapes and gardens.

Cyril Greenland, M.Sc., Ph.D., Professor Emeritus, School of Social Work, McMaster University: President, Museum of Mental Health Services (Toronto) Inc.

Edna Hudson is current president of the Toronto branch of Architectural Conservancy. She is a retired engineer.

Christine I.M. Johnston is a retired social worker and former Historian and Archivist of the First Unitarian Congregation of Toronto. She has recently published a biography of Joseph Workman. She lives in Victoria, British Columbia

Alec Keefer is a local historian. He is former President of
Architectural Conservancy of Ontario, and of the Toronto branch

Shirley Morriss is an independent researcher in Canadian architectural
history. She edited *The Journal of John George Howard, 1833-49*
for the Ontario Heritage Foundation.

Douglas Scott Richardson is Professor of Fine Art at the University of
Toronto.

John Sewell was first elected to Toronto City Council in 1969 and
served as mayor from 1978 to 1980. He is a journalist and com-
mitted social reformer.